THE WORLD'S
GREATEST
DISASTERS

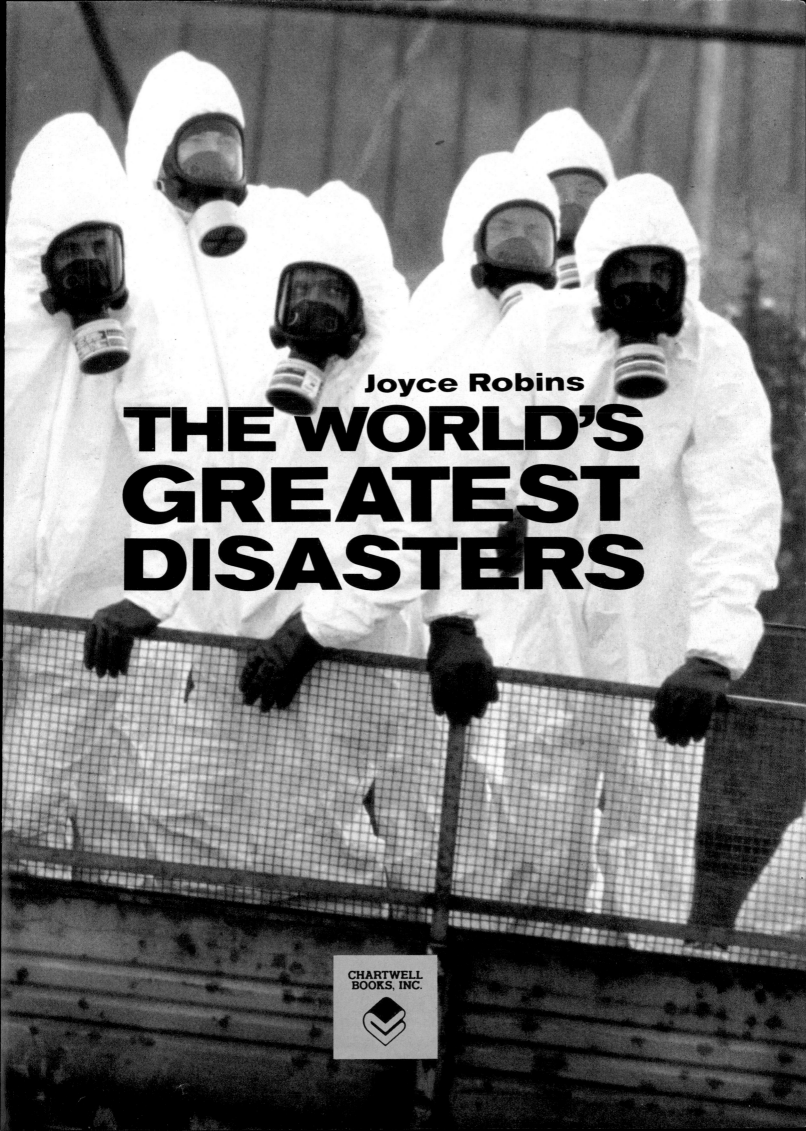

Joyce Robins

THE WORLD'S GREATEST DISASTERS

CHARTWELL
BOOKS, INC.

This 1990 edition published by
Chartwell Books Inc.,
A Division of Book Sales Inc.,
110 Enterprise Avenue, Secaucus,
New Jersey 07094

© Copyright The Hamlyn Publishing Group Limited 1990

ISBN 1-55521-566-1

Produced by Mandarin Offset
Printed and bound in Hong Kong

Contents

The Moving Land   **6**

Volcanoes: *Pompeii, Krakatoa,*
Twentieth-Century Eruptions   8

Earthquakes: *San Francisco 1906,*
Tokyo 1923, Peru 1970, Mexico 1985,
Armenia, 1988   20

Landslides: *Alaska, Hong Kong, Rio*
de Janeiro, Alberta, Aberfan   32

Man's Inhumanity to Man   **36**

The Spanish Inquisition 15th century   38
The Terror in France 1793-4   40
War in the Trenches 1914-18   42
Josef Stalin's Purges   46
The Holocaust   48
Hiroshima 1945   52
The Biafran Famine 1967-70   56
Pol Pot in Cambodia 1975-79   58
The Beirut Bombings 1983   60
The Peking Massacre 1989   64

Catastrophes of Nature   66

The Black Death 1346-50   68
Famine in Ireland 1846-49   70
The Dust Bowl 1930s   72
The Flu Epidemic 1918-19   74
Floods: *China's Yellow River, The Mississippi, Florence*   75
Storms: *Long Island and New England Hurricane 1938, Honduras Hurricane 1974*   80
Tornadoes of the American Midwest 1974   82
More Monster Storms   84
Drought: *USA, Africa*   88
AIDS   92

Man-Made Disasters   94

The Wall Street Crash 1929   96
The Great Depression 1930s   99
The Tragedy of the Thalidomide Babies   102
Chemical Death Clouds: *Seveso 1976, Bhopal 1984*   104
The Jonestown Suicides 1978   108
Trouble in Space 1967, 1971, 1986   110
Football Tragedies 1964, 1971, 1985   114
Nuclear Accidents 1957, 1979, 1986   118
Bursting Dams 1889, 1963   122
Oil Spills: *Torrey Canyon 1967, Amoco Cadiz 1978*   124
Alaska Polluted 1989   126

Tragedies of Air, Sea and Rail   128

Sea Disasters: *The Sinking of the Titanic 1912, The Lusitania 1915, The Morro Castle 1934, The Herald of Free Enterprise 1987*   130
Air Disasters: *The Death of the Airships R101 and the Hindenburg, New York Mid-Air Collision 1960, Tenerife Runway Crash 1977, Potomac River Tragedy 1982, Korean 747 Shootdown 1983, Lockerbie Crash 1988*   138
Rail Disasters: *Tay Bridge 1879, Niagara Falls Special 1887, France 1917, Scotland 1915, Mexico 1955, 1972, Japan 1962, Russia 1989*   150

Fires and Explosions   156

The Great Fire of London 1666   158
The Iroquis Theatre 1903   160
The Cocoanut Grove 1942   162
Mining Accidents: *West Virginia 1907, 1968, Illinois 1909, Wales 1913, 1934, Idaho 1972*   163
The Joelma Building 1974   166
The MGM Grand Hotel 1980   168
The Australian Bush Fires 1983   170
Piper Alpha Explosion 1988   172

Disasters in the Making   174

The Ozone Layer   176
The Greenhouse Effect   178
Acid Rain   182
Deforestation   186

Index   190
Acknowledgements   192

The Moving Land

There are times when the forces deep within the earth remind us of their immense power; earthquakes and volcanoes have demonstrated their savage force throughout history. Tremors from below the ground can topple buildings, carve great gashes in the landscape and bring in their wake tidal waves, fires and destructive mud slides.

Scientists are able to monitor earthquakes and volcanoes more closely than ever before, but in spite of all their expertise, predictions are still too inexact to be of much practical use. Those who live in earthquake zones, such as on the San Andreas fault running through the major cities of California, or who farm the fertile slopes of Vesuvius, develop a fatalistic acceptance of the ever-present threat of disaster.

Volcanoes

The Fall of Pompeii

Volcanoes have existed for as long as the earth itself and their potential for destruction is enormous. They may lie dormant for centuries only to erupt with terrifying fury as tremendous pressure from deep within the earth forces molten rock, or magma, through a crack in the earth's crust. It was such an explosion that destroyed the cities of Pompeii and Herculaneum, killing an estimated 20,000 people.

Volcanologists believe that the history of eruptions of Mount Vesuvius, near Naples in Italy, stretches back for 12,000 years but in AD 79 the inhabitants of the flourishing commercial centre on the Bay of Naples believed that the volcano was extinct. Though they had experienced several violent earth tremors, they did not recognize this as one of the signs of impending explosion and the eruption of August 24 caught them tragically unprepared.

Pliny the Younger witnessed the events of the next two terrible days from the nearby port of Misenum, and gave a firsthand account of them in letters to the historian, Tacitus. The first intimations of disaster came with a huge dark cloud rising from Vesuvius: 'It's shape and appearance suggested nothing so much as a pine tree. Hurled into the air like a great tree trunk, it opened out into branches rising, I suppose, under the first force of the blast. Then, perhaps because its force was exhausted, or even because its own weight was far too much for it, it spread out.'

That was only the beginning of the horror. Soon hot ash and pumice stone began to rain down on Pompeii and poisonous gas was released into the air. Only one in four of the population managed to escape. Most were buried alive by hot ash or suffocated in their homes by sulphurous fumes; some were crushed to death as the roofs of buildings collapsed under the weight of rock and ash.

Pliny recounts how his uncle, Pliny the Elder, sailed towards Pompeii soon after the first signs of the eruption appeared only to find that he was unable to land, as the shoreline was littered with fallen rock. He decided instead to rescue a friend living at Stabiae, further along the coast, but before they could make their escape, they collapsed and died, overcome by the poisonous fumes.

Meanwhile, winds were spreading the danger towards Misenum and Pliny the Younger fled with his mother and other refugees towards open country. 'Behind us,' he wrote, 'a thick and ominous smoke was spreading over the earth. It followed us like a flood . . . We were enveloped by night. It was not the dark of a moonless or cloudy night but the darkness of a sealed room. Only the shrill cries of women, the wailing of children and the shouting of men could be heard.' Ash fell so heavily on them that they had to keep shaking themselves vigorously to avoid being weighed down and buried beneath the weight.

The rain of ash and cinders continued for two days. By then the entire city was buried beneath what looked like a blanket of grey snow. Survivors hoping to salvage possessions or retrieve the bodies of relatives soon gave up the

Above: Vesuvius in eruption is a spectacular sight.
Right: This 18th century drawing by Piranesi, coloured by J.L. Dupréz, shows its terrifying power.

attempt and the site was abandoned.

Herculaneum, a small coastal town to the west of Pompeii, was also obliterated by the eruption. Though it escaped the dust and fumes, heavy rains brought down an avalanche of volcanic mud from the slopes of Vesuvius, burying the town to a depth of 18m (60ft).

The ruins were to lie undisturbed for more than 1,500 years. In the 16th century labourers building an aqueduct dug up coins and jewellery near the site of Pompeii but no further investigations were made until 1748 when a buried wall was discovered and the Bourbon rulers of Naples ordered excavations which revealed parts of the city, while any art treasures uncovered disappeared into the family's private vaults. It was in 1861 that systematic excavations were begun under the directorship of archaeologist Giuseppe Fiorelli and the city was resurrected street by street. After decades of this painstaking work, Pompeii emerged with enough of its ancient splendour to give a unique glimpse of the life and death of the 1900-year-old city.

Bodies which had decomposed had left impressions within the enveloping ash, and plaster casts taken from the cavities give a vivid picture of the last moments of many of the inhabitants: those who died in the streets, their hands over their mouths as they choked on the fumes, a whole family clinging together in the cellars of their home, a pregnant woman lying on her stomach in an attempt to protect her unborn child.

Many of the doors of the houses were left open as the owners fled in panic; others were firmly bolted in the expectation of a quick return. Pots and pans still stood on the hearths, 81 carbonized loaves remained in the oven where they had been baking before the eruption and a pile of coins stood on the counter at the inn, next to the row of drinking vessels. In the luxurious house of Lucius Cecilius Jucundus, 153 documents written on waxed tablets, recording loans, purchases and receipts, were found. Wall mosaics, statues, gardens and fountains and elaborate public buildings bear witness to a prosperous, artistic city. The names of prostitutes inscribed over the door of the brothel and the list of debts on the wall of the gambling house show the seamier side of life.

Excavations at Herculaneum were more difficult, partly because a modern city stood on the same site and partly because the hardened mud surface above it was more difficult to penetrate successfully than the ash of Pompeii. A system of tunnels was used to explore the buried sections of the town but many of the buildings and artifacts excavated had been badly damaged by the mud.

Pompeii and Herculaneum are now both major Italian tourist attractions; so, too, is Vesuvius. People still live and work around the foot of Vesuvius, growing crops and vines on the fertile slopes, but the volcano is still capable of demonstrating its power. Since AD 79 it has erupted 40 times. In 1631, 18,000 people were killed; in 1906 several towns were obliterated. The most recent eruption was in 1944 and experts fear that it is only a matter of time before another explosion.

In the house of Orpheus, a faithful guard dog was suffocated by the falling ash, which hardened to preserve the shape of the animal's body perfectly.

The ruins of Pompeii were excavated in 1861, giving a detailed picture of the life and death of the prosperous ancient city. Among the splendid remains are the Forum and the Arch of Caligula.

The Big Bang at Krakatoa 1883

The Krakatoa group of islands lay between the larger Indonesian islands of Java and Sumatra. Krakatoa itself was 9 km (5½ miles) long, with a string of volcanic cones running from north to south, surrounded by lush tropical vegetation; two smaller islands, Danan and Perbeowetan, were the result of ancient volcanic eruptions dating back nearly one million years.

Seismic activity began in the area in the autumn of 1880, with a succession of earthquakes following over the next three years until 20 May 1883, when a series of volcanic explosions were heard up to 160 km (100 miles) away. From the crater of Perboewetan a great column of steam and ash rose 11 km (7 miles) into the air. As the first explosion died away there was a second, then a third and by early August observers reported that three vents were in active eruption and a dozen more were showing signs of activity.

On 26 August, the giant volcano of Krakatoa itself came to life, with eruptions every few minutes so that the sound was like one thunderous roar. On the morning of 27 August came four vast explosions, one after the other, so powerful that Australians over 3,000 km (2,000 miles) away were woken by a noise like rock-blasting and the noise was heard 4,800 km (3,000 miles) away on Rodriguez Island in the Indian Ocean. The explosion which came at 10.02 hours is considered to be the biggest bang in recorded history.

The islands themselves were uninhabited but 36,000 people died as 38 metre (125 ft) waves called *tsunamis* smashed across the coasts of Java and Sumatra, sweeping away 300 towns and villages in their horrifying path. The effects were felt as far away as San Francisco and the English Channel, where unusually high water levels were recorded. Great chunks of volcanic rock were scattered over 1,500 km (930 miles) of ocean, causing hazards to shipping for months to come. A dark cloud rose 80 km (50 miles) over the site of the volcano. Fine dust discharged into the upper atmosphere travelled right round the world and the results were experienced for several years: a cooling of temperatures as the dust blocked the sun's rays, and magnificent red sunsets throughout the Far East and as far afield as London and America's west coast.

Volcanic activity continued for 33 hours from the time of the first great explosion. When it was over, the northern half of Krakatoa was gone; a 300 metre (1,000 ft) underwater crater now replaced the larger part of the island. Danan and Perboewetan had both disappeared; in all, 5,600 million cubic metres (7,325 million cubic yards) of rock had been blasted out of the sea.

However, Krakatoa refused to die. Over the next 40 years or so, there were periodic roars and rumbles and in January 1925 the peak of a small volcanic cone appeared out of the water. It grew with periodic eruptions until in October 1952 it rose to 60 metres (200 ft). Since then it has grown a further 30 metres (100 ft). It has been named Anak Krakatoa – 'the child of Krakatoa'.

Left: Krakatoa pictured in the early stages of eruption in May 1883 when vast columns of ash and steam rose high into the air, heralding months of powerful activity, vast explosions and tidal waves. Below: an aerial view of the great eruption.

Twentieth-Century Eruptions

The first massive explosion of this century, on the Caribbean island of Martinique, was to wipe out an entire city, leaving only two survivors out of a population of 28,000. St Pierre, a favourite spot for rich French holidaymakers, nestles at the foot of the island's highest peak, Mont Pelée, known as the 'bald mountain' because of the volcanic peak rising up from the luxuriant forest. Inhabitants and holidaymakers alike had few worries about the volcano, although there had been a minor explosion 50 years before.

Then, in April 1902, following a series of earth tremors that did little more than rattle crockery, there were explosions in the secondary crater and ash began to fall on the town, bringing with it the overpowering smell of sulphur. Birds and animals sickened and died and the townspeople, unable to breathe properly, sealed themselves inside their houses. The governor of Martinique arrived in the town to appoint a commission to assess the situation. Astonishingly, the commission reported that there was no immediate danger and the governor, worried that his voters might leave before the elections planned for 10 May, concentrated on calming anxieties and convincing people that they should stay where they were. Several thousand people from the northern half of the island, which was already covered in a blanket of grey ash, poured into the city. Mont Pelée rumbled ominously, belching out great clouds of steam.

On 5 May an avalanche of mud from a boiling lake on the

mountain cascaded down the slopes, carrying away everything in its path, sweeping away a sugar mill and killing 100 people. Panic spread through St Pierre but when people tried to flee, the governor stationed troops on the road to stop them. Three days later the side of the mountain exploded and a killer hurricane of white-hot particles and fiery gasses raced down on the town. The temperature of the blast, believed to be around 1,000°C (1,800°F) is high enough to melt glass, twist steel and turn wood to charcoal. As many as 34,000 people died almost instantaneously and within three minutes the town was reduced to charred rubble; so little remained that when rescuers moved in, they were unable to identify many of the best-known streets.

Experts were unable to explain the survival of a 28-year-old shoemaker Léon Compére-Leandre who was sitting on his doorstep when the explosion occurred. 'All of a sudden I felt a terrible wind blowing, the earth began to tremble and the sky suddenly became dark . . . I felt my arms and legs burning, also my body . . . Crazed and almost overcome, I threw myself on a bed, inert and awaiting death.' Later his senses returned and he was able to reach the next village. Though he had seen everyone around him dying, some strange fluke had preserved his lungs from fatal damage.

Left: An artist's view of the scene in the harbour of St Pierre, 48 hours after the town was devastated by the eruption of Mont Pelée. Below: One of the two townspeople who miraculously survived the disaster.

Left: Experts had been predicting the eruption of the US volcano, Mount St Helens, for several years and it was recorded in detail. Above: Douglas firs were flattened and burned over a vast area of forest.

The only other survivor was Auguste Ciparis, a 25-year-old Negro dock worker who was under sentence of death and confined to a cell with thick walls, a tiny window and a solid door, so low that it could only be entered on all fours. Though he was badly burned and lay for three days without food and water before rescuers reached him, he lived and was subsequently reprieved.

The most carefully monitored and best-recorded eruption ever was probably the explosion of Mount St Helens in Washington State on 18 May 1980. The mountain, born some 40,000 years ago and called Fire Mountain by the North American Indians, had erupted only five times in 280 years. Scientists had been predicting for several years that the 2,900 m (9,500 ft) mountain was likely to erupt violently but the nearest estimate they could give was that it would probably happen before the year 2000.

When the danger signs began to show in late March 1980, as the volcano began to simmer, emergency warnings were issued, 1,000 people were evacuated and no-go areas were established to keep everyone well clear of danger. A fracture nearly 5 km (3 miles) long appeared across the summit and a huge bulge appeared on the north face, swelling to 98 m (320 ft) as thousands of tons of molten rock moved within the mountain. Nationwide publicity roused public interest and people flocked to the area in the hope of seeing a close-up of the eruption. Some disregarded all warnings and blockades and paid for their foolhardy behaviour with their lives.

On the morning of 18 May 1980, the Government Geological Survey base received a sudden, urgent message from scientist David Johnston, who was manning an observation post on the north face. 'This is it,' he told them, 'The mountain's going.' A moment later he was dead, caught in the blast of a shattering explosion. An avalanche of ice and rock boulders cascaded downwards, ice melted by the heat created a 48 km (30 mile) wide mudflow. For nine hours the volcano gushed forth molten rock, scalding ash and choking fumes.

In spite of the emergency procedures 60 people died. As far as 16 km (10 miles) away, people were blasted out of their beds. An enormous cloud of ash was blown east and south by strong winds and towns in Idaho and Montana were brought to a standstill as grey ash blanketed them and snowploughs were summoned to clear the roads for emergency services. Within three days the ash cloud had crossed north America and in 17 days it had travelled right round the world.

An estimated 2,000,000 animals and birds were destroyed and hundreds of square kilometres of forest were flattened. Eleven days after the disaster, rescue worker Robert Wead said: 'The area looks like a nuclear wasteland. Trees and vegetation are laid out flat – singed, burned, steaming, sizzling. President Carter declared a Federal emergency to clear the way for government aid.

Volcanologists hope that close observations of modern eruptions like St Helens will help in work towards better understanding of volcanoes and more accurate prediction of future eruptions but they are still a long way from discovering ways of curbing the destructive force of these fiery mountains. When the Nevada del Ruiz volcano in northern Colombia erupted for the first time in 400 years in November 1985, it claimed the lives of up to 25,000 people as the intense heat melted ice and snow, engulfing two towns in a sea of mud. Armero, 48 km (30 miles) from the volcano, was almost obliterated and hundreds died in their beds, engulfed in a 4.5 m (15 ft) layer of ash and mud. One 12-year-old girl, still buried up to her armpits two days after the quake, gave a brave thumbs-up sign to photographers but she died a day later, before she could be freed.

Below: When Nevada del Ruiz erupted in Colombia, hundreds were trapped in the wreckage of their homes or buried in a sea of mud. Right: Most of the urgent rescue work had to be undertaken in helicopters.

Earthquakes

San Francisco 1906

In the early morning of 18 April 1906, the inhabitants of San Francisco heard a low rumbling, roaring sound. This was the first indication of the colossal earthquake which was to follow. San Francisco's position on the great rupture known as the San Andreas fault meant that its citizens had experienced earthquakes before, the most recent in 1898 and 1900, but this was to be far more severe. Its tremors were felt from Oregon to Los Angeles, a distance of more than 1,000 km (620 miles).

There were three shocks separated by a few seconds, of which the third was by far the greatest. Buildings swayed and tipped, masonry and glass showered down into the streets, chimneys collapsed, church bells clanged wildly. Tramlines snapped under the pressure and reared up from the road like great metal snakes, short-circuiting in blinding sparks as overhead cables fell on them. Thousands of terrified people fled into the streets in their night clothes.

The quake brought its horrors and its humour. One man, lying in his lodging house bed, watched a gap widen in the ceiling. A child's foot appeared then, as the building shifted, the gap snapped closed and the foot was severed, dropping down in a stream of blood. The luxurious Palace Hotel had as one of its guests the great Caruso, who was to sing *Carmen* with the Metropolitan Opera. As the hotel began to shake, Caruso flung open a window and sang a few notes to make sure that his voice was unaffected. Then he left the building and sat on his suitcase in the middle of the street until he was taken to safety. He vowed that he would never come back to San Francisco, and he never did.

Below and right: The San Francisco earthquake and fire of 1906 left fine mansions, hotels and office buildings as piles of rubble. More than 28,000 buildings were destroyed and 200,000 people were homeless, leaving an enormous task of rebuilding.

Left: Some of the town's inhabitants watched the fire raging from a safe vantage point on Russian Hill. Many lost all they possessed in the disaster. Above: It took four days for the fires to burn themselves out, leaving gaunt and blackened remains.

Many fine mansions toppled into ruin; others were left leaning at an angle of 15 degrees from the vertical. The worst effects of the quake were seen in the downtown area, near the site of the original Spanish settlement, Mission Dolores. In Market Street, which divided the wealthy northern half of the city from the poorer southern section, most of the buildings had been shaken to pieces. The newly built City Hall was supposed to be shock-proof but the dome and the gaunt outline of the steel-framed tower were all that survived. However, the loss of life was comparatively small and most people were congratulating themselves on surviving and, as they salvaged bits and pieces from their homes and began cooking breakfast in the street, they reassured one another that things could have been worse.

They bargained without the fire. At first it was dozens of small fires, started where stoves had been left burning or where electric wires had been wrenched free by the tremors. Any stray spark ignited the gas escaping from fractured mains. Four hours after the quake, a woman cooking breakfast, not realizing that her chimney had been destroyed, started the huge 'Ham and Eggs Fire' which was to destroy hundreds of buildings.

The fire service, with only 38 horse-drawn fire engines to cope with 52 fires, was overwhelmed. Water mains on the outskirts of the town fractured, leaving the firemen without water to put out the flames, except for an occasional artesian well and sea water from the bay. Frantic restaurant owners used gallons of wine from their cellars to save their buildings.

Three horror-filled days followed, as winds fanned the flames into an inferno that raged out of control. One survivor described the scene from a hilltop: 'Looking down we saw the great tide of fire roaring in the hollow, burning so steadily yet so fast that it had the effect of immense deliberation, roaring on towards miles of uninhabited dwellings so lately emptied of life that they appeared consciously to

await their immolation.' The whole of Chinatown was reduced to ashes and the homes of the millionaires, on Nob Hill, were all ablaze. The fire service attempted to hold back the fire by dynamiting buildings to create fire breaks but they had so little experience of explosives that they frequently made matters worse. Dynamited buildings blew outwards instead of collapsing and the flaming debris started yet more fires.

Many people were burned to death as they lay trapped in the rubble, including 80 guests in one hotel. 200,000 homeless citizens poured into the large Golden Gate Park, where 23 babies were born on the grass in a single night. Volunteers fought to keep escape routes to embarkation points free from flames, while the Navy ferried thousands of refugees across the Bay to the safety of Oakland. The commander of the federal troops, drafted in to help, wired Washington: 'San Francisco practically destroyed. You cannot send too many tents and rations. 200,000 homeless.'

New problems added to the city's plight. Looters began to plunder the stores and wrecked homes and the mayor was forced to issue a stern proclamation: 'The Federal Troops, the members of the Regular Police Force and all Special Police Officers have been authorized to KILL any and all persons found engaged in looting or in the Commission of Any Other Crime.' Fear of possible epidemics such as cholera led to street signs like : 'Sewers blocked. Don't use toilets. Epidemic threatened. Obey orders or get shot.'

By the fourth day, Saturday 21 April, the fires were burning themselves out but already nearly 500 blocks had been destroyed, and the death toll had risen to nearly 700. But San Francisco is proud to call itself 'the city that knows how' and the rebuilding programme was prompt and impressive. Even while the fires still raged, orders for new equipment including tram lines were being placed. Within two days enough rail track had been repaired to enable visitors from other states to return home. Within two weeks, electricity was restored. Within three years, more than one third of the city had been rebuilt, with many of the new buildings designed to be earthquake and fire resistant. By 1911 when Congress approved San Francisco as the location for a massive world's fair to commemorate the opening of the Panama Canal, no trace of the disaster remained.

The threat of San Francisco's position on the San Andreas fault remains. The fault runs from Cape Mendocino, to the north of San Francisco, across the Golden Gate and through the centre of the peninsula on which the city stands. After that it runs south-eastwards to the hill country behind Los Angeles and on into the Gulf of California. The land mass along the fault shifts frequently, though movements have never again been as severe as that of 1906. Though many of the specially designed buildings of San Francisco are expected to survive future quakes, high-rise blocks present a new danger, as sheets of glass would fall from thousands of shattered windows and the city's many elevated freeways would not withstand a severe tremor. Seismologists believe that a quake on the scale of 1906 could result in 23,000 deaths and they predict that the greatest damage would be seen in the reclaimed land of the city's Bay area.

Tokyo 1923

The densely-populated islands of Japan suffer the onslaught of 15 per cent of all the seismic energy released in the world. Most of the 1,000 or so tremors to affect Japan every year do little serious damage but the three massive shocks that struck Tokyo and Yokohama in 1923 brought deadly destruction. The quake began shortly before noon on Saturday, 1 September, with a full five minutes of shaking. Great chasms opened up in the streets, swallowing up people and vehicles alike, then closing over them. Tokyo's tallest building, 12 storeys high, swayed backwards and forwards before folding at the eighth floor and crashing down. Fire followed almost immediately and, fanned by a strong wind, the flames swept hungrily through the narrow streets of the city. Thousands of people made for the river in search of safety, only to jam the wooden bridges and perish as these caught fire. Others jumped into canals where they stood for hours, only to be found too late with their heads burned beyond recognition, while the submerged part of their bodies remained intact. Others had sought refuge in Tokyo park but freak conditions whipped up a fire cyclone so fierce that it hurled victims high in the air, then flung their charred remains back to the ground.

By the next morning some 300,000 buildings had burned down and two thirds of the Japanese capital was reduced to ashes. As the ground still trembled with aftershocks, many people wandered amid the rubble with the names of missing relatives hung on placards round their necks because they were too parched to speak. The worst damage was in the older, downtown area of the city with the newer, residential sections on high ground to the west coming through almost unscathed. The brand new 250-room Imperial Hotel, designed by the great American architect Frank Lloyd Wright on the theory that shallow foundations over soft earth would withstand earthquakes and allow the hotel to 'float' on the mud below, stood above the ruins, apparent intact. At first this was hailed as a triumph, but the hotel was to sink further and further into the mud over the years, before being demolished in 1968.

The modern port of Yokohama, to the south of the city, suffered appalling damage. The first enormous shock threw the American hospital, with all its inmates, from the cliffs above the town; then the quays buckled, the streets tore apart, and oil tanks ripped open. Most of the buildings, made of wood, smashed like matchsticks and immediately caught fire from the coals of overturned stoves. As the second and third shocks followed, people massed on the shore, crowding onto small boats, only to find a blazing oil slick heading towards them across the water. Many were burned to death but 12,000 were picked up by the *Empress of Australia*, which was being drawn by tugs out of the bay.

The final death toll from Tokyo and Yokohama was 140,000, with a further 100,000 badly injured. More than 2,000,000 lost their homes and hundreds of thousands fled to relatives in the countryside. Those who remained huddled in tents and existed on a handful of rice a day while the rescue services fought to restore some semblance of normality.

Following the disaster, Japan became one of the world leaders in learning how to combat the effects of earthquakes, though many of the grand schemes for buildings that would withstand future quakes were abandoned under the pressure to rehouse the city's inhabitants as

quickly as possible. Tokyo has specially trained earthquake teams, a 10-day supply of water in quake-resistant tanks and well-protected stocks of food and blankets. However, experts say that even reasonable safety from earthquakes has not yet been achieved — and may never prove possible.

Left: A street in the business district of Yokohama shows the savagery of the 1923 earthquake. The wheels on the left are the remains of a handcart. Below: A department store in the Fukui area, jarred out of position by the quake, leans dangerously.

Peru 1970

The US Geological Survey called the quake of 1970 that shook 965 km (600 miles) of the Peruvian coastline and a vast hinterland, leaving some 50,000 dead and 800,000 homeless, 'the most destructive historic earthquake in the western hemisphere.' Though the recorded history of earthquakes in Peru goes back to 1619, so that Peruvians are always aware of the possibility and have learned to accept minor quakes philosophically, no one could have been prepared for anything on such an enormous scale.

It came on a Sunday afternoon, soon after many Peruvians had settled down to hear the World Cup soccer match in their homes. Twenty-three minutes after the start of the match, the ocean bed west of the busy fishing port of Chimbote cracked and the resulting quake measured almost eight on the Richter scale. The shock

reached out across the land to both north, south and east.

News of the extent of the catastrophe was slow to emerge; communications were severed, roads were impassable and a combination of mist and dust prevented helicopter pilots from assessing the damage. At Chimbote, 70 per cent of buildings had been destroyed and there and in the other coastal towns, thousands had perished. In the high mountains, the ice cap of Mt Huascaran had collapsed, beginning an avalanche of several thousand tonnes of rock which came pouring down the valley at 320 km (199 miles) an hour. The town of Yungay, a flourishing ski resort, and part of the neighbouring Ranrahirca disappeared under the roaring rocks. Only 92 of Yungay's inhabitants survived; they had taken refuge on the top of Cemetery Hill, on the edge of town. A dozen more towns, each with 2,000-3,000 inhabitants, were now nothing but heaps of rocks.

The death toll mounted steeply because of the impossi-

Left: The Peruvian town of Yungay was wiped off the map by the great fall of rock and ice following the 1970 earthquake. Only Cemetery Hill, topped by a statue of Christ, escaped. Above: The statue of Christ stands unscathed amid the piles of rubble.

bility of getting help quickly to the remote and inaccessible regions of the Andes. The resources of relief workers were stretched to breaking point and freezing rain hampered their efforts so that it was days before the first help arrived. Hundreds of thousands of Indian peasants were marooned in the remains of their villages without food or shelter for a week. Hungry, shivering survivors made for the nearest towns only to find, like the two injured policemen who staggered hopefully into Huaraz three days after the earthquake, that the townspeople were in desperate need themselves. It was to be months before the inhabitants of the steep Andean villages could begin to recover

from the effects of 'the giant's hand', as they called it. In many cases their deep distrust of strangers hampered the work of helpers who found that the villagers were hiding the injured and orphaned from them.

Even on the coastal plain, where rescue operations began speedily, the task often seemed impossibly great. In Chimbote, five days after the earthquake, rescue workers were still digging bodies out of the rubble. Many people preferred to sleep in the open, or in shelters made from harmless rushes rather than trust themselves to any form of building and some could not bear to sleep at all, terrified that another quake would come.

Gradually the 'uncomprehending silence' which one observer reported as settling over the ruined towns turned to the noise and bustle of people determined to rebuild their lives. When, on 2 June, Peru won a World Cup match against Bulgaria, red and white Peruvian flags were planted on the piles of rubble that had once been houses.

Mexico 1985

A full week after the massive earthquake that destroyed one third of Mexico City in September 1985, rescue workers were still digging out survivors from the rubble of fallen buildings and amazing scenes at the city's central hospital caught the attention of the world. The hospital had toppled in the quake and the fire that followed ignited cotton wool, surgical spirit and other medical supplies. There were more than 1,000 people in the building at the time; hundreds died trapped between collapsed floors, many of those who survived the quake itself were asphyxiated as the fire took hold. Victims included the heads of surgery, intensive care and obstetrics, who died at their posts and at least 150 mothers and babies, though 58 newborn babies were found alive in the maternity ward nursery. After seven days of digging, when it seemed impossible that more survivors could be found, a premature baby, badly dehydrated but unhurt, was brought out to a chorus of wild cheers.

Towns in three provinces – Colima, Guerrero and Michaocan – were devastated by the earthquake, which measured 8.1 on the Richter scale and was felt in Houston, Texas, 1,200 km (745 miles) to the north and in Guatemala City, 1,000 km (621 miles) to the south. At Ciudad Guzman, in Colima, 40 per cent of the houses were destroyed and at Atentique, in Jalisco, part of the mountain broke away and killed scores of peasants who were just getting ready for a day's work.

'Mexico has been hit with the force of a mighty blow from hell', said one TV reporter. In Mexico City, with its 18,000,000 people, the hardest hit areas were the historic town centre, the east side and the southern district round the National Medical Centre. Schools, cathedrals and hotels were levelled; thick dust clouds surrounded collapsed buildings, broken glass and chunks of cement littered the streets. An eight storey apartment building folded into a heap less than two storeys high, with large sections of its roof still intact. Many of the buildings still standing leaned at an angle of 75°.

The government appealed for blood donors as troops patrolled the streets after reports of looting by thieves posing as rescue workers. The smell of rotting bodies was everywhere and the health authorities did their best to fumigate the ruined buildings in an attempt to prevent an outbreak of disease. Medical teams were innoculating people against tetanus and typhoid in the streets. Unidentified bodies were laid out on a baseball pitch on the edge of the city but those that were not claimed within three days were buried in mass graves as big as houses.

All the while, the rescue efforts continued with the aid of teams of dogs from the United States and Europe, trained to sniff out any survivors still buried. It took two days of digging to liberate a young medical student who had been tending a patient at the time of the quake. A 22-year-old woman was entombed for seven days before rescuers got through; a team of seven Miami firemen, helped by Mexican miners, dug three tunnels through the ruins before they could make contact and finally pulled her out through a 12 m (40 ft) passage.

An eight-day-old baby was found alive after lying beside the body of his dead mother for 103 hours. Experts, asked why so many babies managed to survive for long periods without food, water or care, explained that babies lack the 'psychological factor'. They do not use up life-saving calories in a state of fear and stress, as adults do.

Right: Many buildings in Mexico City became grave-sites when the aftershock hit. Below: A rescue worker with a sniffer dog searches for survivors.

Armenia 1988

The earthquke that struck Armenia on 7 December 1988 had been half-expected by Soviet scientists, who had been predicting that a major quake was overdue in the area. When it came it was the most powerful tremor in 80 years, measuring 9 on the Richter scale, and because quakes in Armenia occur at relatively shallow depths, making cities here particularly susceptible to damage, the results were appalling. Leninakan, Armenia's second city with a population of 300,000, was 48 km (30 miles) from the epicentre and there 80 per cent of buildings were destroyed. Many high-rise blocks, made from pre-fabricated panels, were reduced to rubble and became graves for hundreds of people. The town of Spitak, with a population of 20,000, was complately flattened. One survivor said simply: 'Spitak has perished – it is an ex-city, it is not possible to describe the dimensions of the catastrophe.'

At first, rescue workers were left to claw at the rubble with their bare hands; there were no cranes, no lifting gear, no lights. The official newspaper *Pravda* commented critically on the absence of trained rescue units: 'There are a dozen observers for every man working, all giving advice instead of clearing up the rubble themselves . . . Hours were lost – and that means lives.'

Reporters who reached Leninakan soon after the tremor were met by terrible scenes: 'Sobbing, helpless people were climbing among the debris of homes, from which heart-rending cries for help could be heard. Powerless to do anything, those left free and alive rushed madly to and fro.' There was a shortage of everything from bulldozers to blankets and piles of rubble blocked the streets, so that ambulances were unable to get through to collect the injured.

Soviet President Gorbachev cut short a triumphant visit to the United States, expressing his 'deep gratitude and

Above: Tens of thousands died when the worst quake for 80 years hit Armenia – the poor construction methods used in the cities contributed to the high death toll. Right: Fenya Apinyan, who lost both her husband and her son, sits mourning in the ruins.

profound appreciation' for all the emergency help promised. Once the relief operation was under way, it turned into the biggest effort ever mounted in the Soviet Union. Specialist helpers flew in from the major western countries; in every Soviet city people queued to give blood, clothing and money.

The skies over Leninakan were full of planes bringing troops, engineers, medical supplies and personnel. Another crushing blow came when, five days after the earthquake, a military transport aircraft collided with a helicopter and crashed, killing 78 Russian servicemen who were being ferried in as part of the rescue effort. A second relief aircraft, a Yugoslav air force transport bringing medical supplies, crashed soon afterwards killing all seven on board.

The official death toll rose to 55,000, though unofficial estimates stand at nearer 100,000. Coffins were stacked along the streets waiting for the bodies as they were dug out and the dead were carried away in a continuous procession. A football pitch was used as a temporary mortuary, where survivors came to try to identify the frozen bodies. Hundreds of thousands of homeless people huddled in tents that offered little protection from sub-zero temperatures. Many commentators believe that the poor construction of buildings in Armenian cities – low grade concrete used in the pre-fabricated sections of high-rise buildings and the lack of steel reinforcement frames – meant that far fewer people trapped inside them had a fair chance of survival than in the earthquake in Mexico three years before.

Landslides

Landslides can be one of the most dangerous of natural disasters; they may come without warning, so fast that there is no time for evacuation or safety measures. Those in their path can be swept away before they realize that danger threatens.

Some major landslides are triggered by seismic activity, like the Good Friday earthquake of 1964 in Anchorage, Alaska, which set off a dramatic landslide at one of the city's smartest housing developments, Turnagain Heights. Here a group of expensive houses was perched on a headland that was not stable enough to withstand the stress of a quake. The scientific name for what followed is liquifaction: the layer of wet soil, particularly sand and silt, on which the cliff rested was turned into a wet, slippery substance by seismic activity and this began to slide down the steep hill to the inlet below, carrying the top layer, with its houses and streets, inexorably with it.

Many residents were at home getting ready for the Easter holiday on a wet, snowy afternoon when they felt their houses buck and twist and heard the sounds of breaking glass and cracking timbers. Trees and fences seemed to rise from the ground, and the ground itself cracked and tilted. As 2.5 km (1.5 miles) of headland slid downwards, 70 homes went with it and houses that had been 30 m (100 ft) above sea level ended up as heaps of timber at the water's edge.

People marooned halfway down the cliff, hanging onto chunks of earth that were still moving, were pulled to safety by neighbours with ropes. One family was less fortunate. A 12-year-old boy managed to get his sister and two brothers out of the house when the quake hit, but once they were outside the ground opened beneath their feet and two of the boys disappeared into the crevasse. Their bodies were never found.

Even heavy rain can bring death and damage where buildings have been constructed on unstable slopes. On the crowded island of Hong Kong far too little attention was paid to the suitability of the ground as more and more high-rise buildings crowded up the steep hillsides from the bay. Tropical vegetation grows rapidly in Hong Kong, giving a false air of stability to the land, but a series of landslides tells a different story.

In 1966, 64 people were killed when part of the hillside was swept away and 8,000 had to be evacuated; then in 1972 a high-rise block of flats collapsed, killing over 70 people, as the ground beneath it slid downhill. The pressure for housing on the island is so great that the authorities were slow to react to calls for additional safety measures, and in 1970, when 500 mm (20 inches) of rain fell in 48 hours, the steady downpour set off a series of landslides which killed 22 people and injured 65. Once again, thousands were rendered homeless while a system of artificial terraces was constructed to minimize the problem in the future.

Below: Homes in Anchorage, Alaska, were damaged when they slid down a hillside. Right: In Hong Kong, British troops search for survivors in the ruins of a 12 storey building after a landslide. A rescue worker uses a torch to cut through iron rods.

In the first three months of 1966, Rio de Janeiro suffered the heaviest rainfall in its history, setting off slides that showed no mercy to the shanty towns crowded on hillsides at the edge of the city. Whole communities were swept away in minutes, with a final death toll of 280. In 1974 the vast cascade of rock and mud that slid down the sides of Quebradablanca Canyon in Columbia onto the busy main highway linking the capital, Bogota, with Villavicencio was so sudden and lethal that it buried six crowded buses and 20 other vehicles, killing over 200 and injuring 100 more.

Local industry precipitated the rockfall at the coal-mining town of Frank in Alberta, Canada in 1903. Mining at the foot of Turtle Mountain had removed major supporting rocks from the valley wall and altered the drainage patterns of the rest. The rock avalanche that half buried the town of Frank killed 70 people and many experts believe that residents there are now in danger of an even greater landslide that could wipe out the town altogether.

Both man and nature had a hand in one of the most notorious of all landslips at the small Welsh village of Aberfan when a slag heap collapsed, engulfing the village school. Among the 147 dead were 116 children, virtually a whole generation of Aberfan schoolchildren. There had been plenty of warnings about the tip, especially after a slide in 1963, but the authorities had taken little notice and debris was still being dumped on the tip when the tragedy occurred.

Left: An aerial view of Aberfan after the mountain of mine waste collapsed down on the village, burying houses, shops and a school under an avalanche of sludge. Below: An army of helpers work tirelessly to clear the debris covering the local school.

The slide, with its 2,000,000 tons of mine waste and thick black sludge, came thundering down at 09.30 on the morning of 21 October 1966, just as the schoolchildren were assembling for roll-call, burying everything to a depth of 14 m (45 ft). More than 2,000 police, firemen and other rescue·workers spent all day and all night tunnelling through the slag in the search for survivors. Some children were rescued by local women who pulled them out of a half-collapsed room at the back of the school but as the first small bodies were carried out of the mud and the extent of the tragedy became clear, experienced reporters and policemen broke down in tears. A *Guardian* reporter wrote: 'It was a day of the most stark and bitter horror. . . The first two bodies found were little girls. They had just entered the rear playground and their hands were still clasped. A teacher was found dead, her body hunched in a corner by a classroom radiator, protecting a group of children huddled round her. But they, too, were dead.'

Ten thousand people attended on 27 October when the first funerals took place and 81 small coffins were laid in two long communal graves. A huge cross made up of wreaths sent from all over the world was laid across them.

The British National Coal Board stated that the cause of the fall was the recent heavy rain, but the Tribunal of Inquiry revealed that an underlying stream had undermined the foundations of the tip and that there had been major mistakes in siting and managing it. The unanimous view was that the 'disaster could and should have been prevented.' In future tips were to be subject to regular inspection and supervision. Although the remains of the tip above Aberfan were declared safe, local people continued to press for its removal and it was taken away two years later so that the new school of Aberfan would never be menaced.

Man's Inhumanity to Man

Some of the most appalling suffering experienced in the world has been inflicted deliberately by those in power on those at their mercy. The western world may have looked on in horror as the Chinese government suppressed student protest, shooting down hundreds of unarmed citizens, but history is littered with examples of man's boundless inhumanity to man. In 15th-century Spain, in Russia under Stalin's rule and in Nazi Germany, the midnight knock has had the same terrifying meaning: arrest, torture and likely death.

Every tyrant, from Robespierre in revolutionary France to Pol Pot in Cambodia, has claimed to be pursuing a vision of a better world, but their fanatical régimes have bred cruelty and terror.

The Spanish Inquisition 15th century

The Inquision in Spain was a powerful political weapon, authorized by Pope Sixtus IV in 1478 when the rule of Ferdinand and Isabella had united Aragon and Castile, to enable them to root out insincere converts to Christianity who might undermine the Catholic faith and threaten the unity of the country. It was aimed mainly at the Jews who had been driven to 'convert' by waves of persecution over the years but who still secretly adhered to Jewish practices, and were seen as a real threat by the ruling aristocracy. They were convinced that only rigorous interrogation would reveal the truth and give heretics the final opportunity to confess and repent.

The initial aims of the Inquisition were soon lost in an orgy of accusation and retribution. Men and women were denounced for not eating pork or for eating meat on the day of abstinence, for having a family gathering on the Jewish sabbath or for smiling when Christ's name was mentioned. They could be arrested in their homes in the middle of the night and languish in prison for months without knowing what charges were laid against them. The accused were never told who the witnesses were or what they had said, so that they often ended up accusing themselves of everything they could think of, in the hope of escaping torture by 'confessing'. Any real attempt at defence was useless; once someone had been arrested, they were assumed to be guilty.

The name of Tomás de Torquemada, the Inquisitor General, became synonymous with fear and persecution. Scores of permanent and temporary tribunals were set up throughout the country, each of them employing hundreds of staff and most of them financed from the confiscated property of the supposed heretics. In some Spanish towns, excitement and fear ran at fever pitch, with neighbours and relatives rushing to accuse one another, so that prisons were packed with people waiting to be interrogated. Though Sixtus IV tried to intervene, he was powerless to stop the worst excesses.

Torturers relied mainly on the rack, the ordeal by water, where litres of water were poured down the prisoner's throat through a funnel, and the *strappado*, where the prisoner's wrists were tied behind his back, then attached to a pulley. He was then hoisted aloft, often with weights attached to his feet. All the time, a clerk would carefully note down every word, every scream uttered by the victim.

Sentence was pronounced on the 'heretics' at the *auto de fé*, a public ceremony with some of the trappings of a carnival. The most important were held in the central square of Madrid before the king and his court, and for twelve hours, prisoner after prisoner was brought forward for sentence. Punishments included imprisonment, confiscation of property, confinement in the galleys and public

Above right: Among the tortures of the Inquisition were the rope and pulley and ordeal by water or fire. Below right: Heretics were burned at the stake in front of a crowd of spectators. Above: A woman condemned to the stake, dressed in the special costume called the *sambenito*.

flogging, with 100 lashes as the usual sentence. Neither young nor old were spared: in Valencia a 13-year-old girl and an 86-year-old man were both sentenced to 100 lashes. As the culmination of the *auto de fé*, heretics who refused to confess were burned at the stake. Historians differ widely in their estimates of how many people were put to death; probably at least 3,000 died in the frenzied early years, before 1550, and perhaps another 1,000 by the time the Inquisition was finally abolished in 1834.

The Terror in France 1793-4

The glorious French Revolution of 1789 declared itself for 'liberty, equality and fraternity', freeing the people from the near-feudal tyranny of the aristocracy. However, less than five years after the declaration of the Rights of Man, the mob was baying for blood. Countering those who argued for moderation, pamphleteer Jean Paul Marat wrote: 'In order to ensure public tranquillity, 200,000 heads must be cut off', and the Committee of Public Safety, headed by Robespierre, set out to annihilate all enemies of the revolution – real or imagined.

Louis XVI had been executed in January 1793. In October it was the turn of his queen, Marie Antoinette, and after that the floodgates were opened. Soon the tum-

brils rolled busily along the road to the guillotine in the Place de la Révolution, now the Place de la Concorde, bringing victims to their deaths. About 3,000 people were executed in Paris alone; the guillotine was such a speedy method of execution that as many as 60 could be dispatched in 54 minutes. The smell of the stale blood that soaked the square was so overwhelming that residents of the nearby Rue Saint-Honoré complained that it was a health hazard.

The executions were a public entertainment; young girls danced behind the tumbrils, Parisian women knitted cosily below the scaffold while their husbands laid bets on who would die first. The English essayist William Hazlitt wrote: 'The shrieks of death were blended with the yell of the assassin and the laughter of the buffoons. Whole families were led to the scaffold for no other crime than their relationship: sisters for shedding tears over the death of

The artist Delacroix depicted Liberty leading the people of France.

The Revolution reached the point of no return when Louis XVI was condemned to the guillotine.

their brothers; wives for lamenting the fate of their husbands; innocent peasant girls for dancing with Prussian soldiers'.

Bodies and heads were stacked into carts and taken to the cemetery where they were stripped and thrown into pits. Even so, the cemeteries were soon full and more had to be opened. In those with clay soil, the ground could not soak up all the blood and bonfires of herbs were burned constantly to kill the smell.

The massacres went on outside Paris, too, where there was a death count of something like 14,000. No one was safe from the Terror. Though aristocrats were the prime targets, 85 per cent of those executed were commoners. Anyone who wanted to settle a score with an old enemy could accuse him of food hoarding or of sneering at the cause of the revolution, and many died simply because they bore the same name as someone who had already

been accused. Sadists in powerful positions indulged their whims at the expense of helpless prisoners. In Nantes the dreaded Jean-Baptiste Carrier had 2,000 people loaded into boats and taken out into the river Loire, stripped and bound together, then drowned. Afterwards the river was so polluted with rotting corpses that fishing was banned.

However, more and more members of the ruling Convention became sickened by the massacres. Though Robespierre insisted: 'At the point where we are now, if we stop too soon we will die. We have not been too severe', the Convention turned against him and on 28 July 1794 he and his aides followed their thousands of victims to the guillotine and, at last, the Terror came to an end.

War in the Trenches 1914-18

World War I was probably the most static war ever fought. For weeks and months on end, millions of men on opposing sides faced one another across a narrow strip of no man's land. They lived in trenches with no shelter from the cold and rain, often knee-deep in water. Battles fought to gain at most a few kilometres of land meant furious bombardments followed by foot soldiers advancing against enemy machine guns, and being mown down by the thousand.

In August 1914, the allies expected a short, decisive war but instead, after the German advance into Belgium, both sides found themselves deadlocked on the western front in a line of trenches that eventually stretched for 725 km (450 miles). On Christmas Day, 1914, British troops in France heard the Germans singing carols in their trenches and the soldiers met in no man's land and exchanged cigarettes. When the news of this reached the military command, such fraternization was strictly forbidden in future and the soldiers went back to shooting each other.

As the war progressed, the horror of the trenches increased. Gas was used by both sides and though it was never a very effective war weapon – changing wind could blow it back on the users – the psychological effects on men confined to holes in the ground was tremendous. Bombardments became fiercer and fiercer as both sides tried to annihilate the enemy forces; more and more men were fed into the war machine although there was nothing but the steadily-mounting death toll to show for it. At the battle of Verdun, the combined casualties of French and German forces numbered 700,000 with no measurable gains on either side.

Immediately afterwards came the battle of the Somme, when wave upon wave of British infantry advanced into the mouths of the enemy guns. Most were killed in the first 90 metres (100 yards) of no man's land; some died before they could leave their own trenches, falling backwards onto others who were still trying to scramble out. On the first day of the attack, 19,000 British soldiers died and 60,000 were wounded. The battle was to rage on for four and a half months. At the end of it all the Allies had managed no significant breakthrough, but had lost more than 600,000 men.

The battles fought around the Belgian town of Ypres left the area a sea of mud and blasted trees. Any soldier who stepped off the duckboards could sink up to his neck in a water-filled shell hole. The last of these battles, at Passchendaele, in 1917, lasted 4 months. Casualties from both sides totalled half a million men.

In 1917 the USA entered the war and the British government was in favour of suspending the offensive on the western front until US soldiers arrived in force. However, the commander-in-chief, Field Marshal Sir Douglas Haig, was still convinced that allied forces could breach the German lines and win by frontal attack. The site chosen for the great offensive was Passchendaele. The assault lasted from late July to November, while heavy rain added to the effects of bombardment and turned the ground into a bog. Soldiers sank up to their waists in mud, guns and tanks stuck fast. It could take 12 men to struggle through the morass with a stretcher so the wounded often lay screaming in the mud until they died. Eight kilometres (five miles) of extra shell-torn territory had cost 300,000 British soldiers and 200,000 Germans.

Passchendaele was the last of the old-style battles, and after the arrival of 1,000,000 American troops in Europe in early 1918 the combined allied effort began to roll back the German front at last.

Below: Gas attacks were among the horrors of war and many young men were blinded by mustard gas as they lay pinned down in their trenches. Right: British troops retreat before a cloud of gas from a German attack, seen as a reddish cloud. Below right: Casualties on both sides were heavy. These young Germans died when Allied troops smashed their machine gun post.

Josef Stalin's Purges

Josef Stalin, the shoemaker's son who played an important role in the Russian Revolution of 1917, rose to absolute power in Russia in 1929. During his rule he was to transform Russia from a backward rural country into one of the world's foremost industrial and military nations but his achievement was bought at a tremendous cost in human life and misery. One of his first moves was to announce a massive agricultural and industrial development programme, the 'second revolution'.

He saw collectivization – the combining of small farms and plots into vast units – as essential for his plan and when he met resistance from the *kulaks*, the better-off peasants, he decided to eliminate them as a class. Many resisted violently, destroying their crops and slaughtering their livestock rather than handing them over. They were met with harsh repression. Evicted at gunpoint, they were either murdered or confined in 'corrective labour camps'. Stalin later told Churchill that 10,000,000 *kulaks* had been killed, commenting 'What is one generation?'

Industrial output rose rapidly, so that between 1932 and 1937 it increased by 14 per cent a year but many of the new coal, iron and steel complexes were built by the forced labour of half-starved, overworked men. Meanwhile, Stalin was tightening his despotic grip on the whole of Russian society. The party and government bureaucracies were purged of 'unreliable' workers, with 164,000 Moscow civil servants sacked within 18 months. Millions of people – writers, office workers, party officials, church members – were arrested and suffered the same fate as the *kulaks*. More than half of the Red Army leaders disappeared. All Communist Party members who might put principles before the new politics of power were eliminated and replaced by those who would obey Stalin blindly. By 1934, the camps were said to contain 10,000,000 people.

The 1930s saw a series of show trials, where Stalin's old revolutionary colleagues found themselves charged with conspiring against the state. Most confessed their 'guilt', probably as a result of torture and threats to their families. The 'Great Terror' lasted until 1939, but by then World War II was on the horizon and Stalin was able to extend his brutal régime to Rumania, Hungary, Poland and Bulgaria. After the Yalta summit agreement between the great powers, 3,000,000 Russian refugees, some of them soldiers who had fought for Hitler, but also many White Russians who had fled from the results of the revolution, were forcibly repatriated. Once they arrived on Russian soil, thousands of helpless hostages were taken straight from the boats to makeshift execution yards and shot; the rest went to a slower death in the camps.

Towards the end of his life, the ruthless tyrant became a prisoner of his own fears, living in terror of betrayal or assassination. His daughter Svetlana described him as being 'as bitter as he could be against the whole world. He saw enemies everywhere. It had reached the point of being pathological, of persecution mania'. By the time of his death in 1953, he had established the Soviet Union as the second most powerful nation in the world, but 20,000,000 lives had been sacrificed in the process. Count Nikolai Tolstoy wrote that throughout the enormous nation, 'scarcely a family had been untouched by tragedy'. As more and more details of his vicious methods were exposed, he was discredited both at home and abroad.

Below: Pro-Stalinist peasants demonstrate their support for collectivization. Their banner reads 'Liquidate the kulaks as a class immediately'. Above right: One of Stalin's committees at work, deciding how many members of the party must be 'purged'.

The Holocaust

Throughout World War II, reports of the Nazi's policy of genocide against the Jews of Europe had been reaching the Allies but they were given little publicity and were often discounted as exaggerated. American and British governments dragged their feet over opening their doors to Jewish refugees, claiming that their arrival might stir up latent anti-semitism. Immigration regulations were strict and, in all, perhaps 200,000 refugees were received into the United States, and some 55,000 into Britain, leaving many would-be immigrants to perish at the hands of the Nazis. It was only when Allied troops opened up the death camps that the full horror of Hitler's 'Final Solution' was revealed and the wholesale extermination of 6,000,000 Jews was documented.

From the moment Hitler came to power in 1933, he began whipping up anti-semitic fervour and instituting anti-Jewish measures. New laws limited the right of Jews to work and imposed extra taxes. The wholesale destruction of Jewish property began on 9 November 1938, the notorious *Kristallnacht*, or 'night of broken glass'. The following year the ghettoes came into being in Poland: the largest was in Warsaw, where 400,000 people were crammed into one section of the city in appalling conditions, forbidden to leave under penalty of death. In the first six months of 1941, 13,000 died of starvation in the Warsaw ghetto.

For the power-crazed Nazi leader, this was only the beginning. At that time, two-thirds of the world's Jewish population lived in Europe and he planned to murder them all, along with gypsies, homosexuals and the mentally ill, all of whom failed to fit in with his grand design of racial superiority. As the German troops invaded the USSR in June 1941, Hitler ordered the implementation of the Final Solution. Hundreds of thousands died in mass killings, often forced to dig their own graves in a quiet spot or woodland, then gunned down as they stood in rows at the edge of the pit.

The official line was that Jews were being deported for

forced labour; when the transports to the specially pre-pared death camps began, they were told that they were to be 'resettled'. Some camps, like Treblinka, Chelmno, Sobibor and Belzec, were set up solely as extermination centres. Others, like Auschwitz, were already in existence as concentration camps, and gas chambers and cremato-ria were built there in late 1942; the crematoria were de-signed to dispose of 2,000 bodies every 24 hours.

It was at Auschwitz that a fast-acting lethal gas, hydro-gen cyanide, was introduced; it was dropped as pellets through grills in the top of the gas chambers. As train loads of Jews arrived at Auschwitz, some were selected for slave labour, others for immediate execution, though the fiction that they were merely being prepared for life in the camp by bathing and delousing was maintained to the end. The victims were stripped, their hair was cut and they were even given soap and towels as they were herded into the gas chambers. Once they were dead their bodies were rifled for the gold in their teeth. Even though reports of the atrocities began to leak out of Germany, the Allied governments consistently rejected calls from Jewish agencies to bomb the railway lines leading to Auschwitz and the gas ovens, though American planes were bomb-ing industrial centres only a few miles away.

The Jews fought back as best they could but the price was high: when a Jewish resistance group in a town near Auschwitz managed to kill 25 Germany soldiers, 250 chil-dren and old people were massacred as a reprisal. When a trainload of Jews on the way to Treblinka turned on their guards, using fence posts as weapons, the SS machine-gunned prisoners and guards alike, killing well over 1,000 in a few minutes. The most famous uprising was in the

Left: Hitler's birthday in 1939 was celebrated in grand style, with the dictator taking the salute as 50,000 soldiers goose-stepped past. Below: Hundreds of thousands of Jews were marched out into the countryside and forced to dig their own graves.

Warsaw ghetto in April 1943 where at one stage the Jewish underground managed to drive the Germans out of the ghetto altogether and halt the mass deportations. However, the German forces returned to burn down the ghetto: more than 56,000 Jews were burned alive, shot as they tried to escape from burning buildings, or deported to Treblinka to be killed.

The Nazis regarded the Jews as vermin, so even those who were not immediately selected for death were subjected to inhuman treatment and cruelty. Many were worked to death, others were tortured for the entertainment of the guards. The commandant of Mauthausen once boasted that he had given his young son 50 Jews for target practice. In many camps doctors performed medical experiments, without anaesthetic, merely to satisfy their curiosity.

Even when the German armies were in retreat, the policy of deportation and killing continued and, as more and more Germans realized that the war was lost, they became obsessional about disposing of all those who could bear witness to their crimes. As the American and British forces advanced, thousands were evacuated from the camps, herded into trains or marched for weeks on end until they died of exhaustion. A death march from Birkenau lasted over six weeks, and less than 1 in 10 of the 3,000 who set out were alive at the end of the journey.

On 4 April 1945, US troops reached the camp at Ohrdruf, where hundreds of Jews had been killed the day before their arrival; the photographs of the piles of emaciated corpses sent shock waves through both the United States and Britain. Worse was to come: at Belsen, the British found several thousand unburied corpses, and at Nordhausen the Americans found hundreds of slave labourers who were no more than human skeletons, the living scarcely distinguishable from the sick and the dead as they lay side by side in the same beds. The last camp liberated by the Americans was Mauthausen, where they discovered 10,000 bodies in a mass grave; more than 30,000 had died there in the previous three months.

The final estimates of the numbers of Jews exterminated included 3,000,000 from Poland, 1¼ million from the Soviet Union and more than 230,000 from Western Europe – in all, the Nazis managed to dispose of two thirds of the 9,000,000 Jews under their control. In spite of all their efforts, something like 300,000 Jews survived the camps though tens of thousands were so weak and sick that they died after the liberation. Between 1944 and 1948 over 200,000 survivors went to Palestine, while 72,000 found a new home in the USA and 16,000 in Canada, though many took years to adjust to normal life again after the horrors they had experienced.

Right: Josef Goebbels was Hitler's right-hand man, the propaganda expert who promoted the idea of Aryan superiority. Far right: When Allied soldiers entered the concentration camps they found horrifying scenes of suffering and death with unburied bodies lying in heaps. Hitler tried to exterminate the entire Jewish race as part of this 'final solution'.

Hiroshima 1945

On 16 July 1945 the atom bomb was successfully tested at Alamogordo, New Mexico. A note was passed to US President Truman, at the Potsdam conference with the Allied leaders, saying simply: 'It's a boy'. Almost immediately afterwards work on assembling 'Little Boy', a uranium bomb, and 'Fat Boy', a plutonium bomb, began on the Pacific airbase of Tinien, ready to attack Japanese cities at the beginning of August. Use of this new weapon, developed as a result of the costly 'Manhattan Project', was presented as an alternative to the proposed invasion of Japan, planned for November. Any such invasion would cost many American lives. The month-long battle for the small island of Iwo Jima in February had cost the US Marines 25,000 casualties and 8,000 Americans died in the three months it took to subdue Okinawa. There were other considerations, too: an invasion would need the co-operation of the Soviet Union and many US officials wanted to make sure that the power of the Soviet Union was not increased by its involvement in the post-war settlement in Japan.

Already a meeting at US military headquarters had discussed whether or not Japanese leaders should be warned of the bombings so that the bombs could act as a demonstration of power without killing large numbers of civilians, who could be evacuated beforehand. However, this was thought far too risky: it would give the Japanese every opportunity to shoot down the bombers and if, for any reason, the bombs failed to perform, the Japanese would win a great propaganda victory. The meeting advised that the bomb should be used as soon as possible, without warning, and that it should be used against a combined military and civilian target. Hiroshima, a city of 245,000 people, an important military base housing 100,000 soldiers and large supply dumps, seemed an ideal choice. It had suffered comparatively little from conventional bombing up to now, another point in its favour as far as the military command was concerned because it meant that the effect of a single atom bomb could be observed more easily.

The Potsdam Declaration demanded unconditional surrender from Japan, warning that 'the only alternative . . . is prompt and utter destruction'. When Japan did not capitulate, the fate of Hiroshima was sealed, and on 6 August a B29 bomber, the *Enola Gay*, dropped its four-and-a-half-ton load, the uranium bomb 'Little Boy'. The crew of the plane saw first an intense glare, then a vast column of smoke rising into the air. The rear gunner, Lieutenant Caron, described it over his intercom: 'It has a fiery red core; a bubbling mass, purple-grey in colour, with that red core . . . Fires are springing up everywhere, like flames shooting out of a huge bed of coals . . . Here it comes, the mushroom shape . . . It's like a mass of bubbling molasses

Right: The mushroom cloud of the bomb dropped on Nagasaki. Far right above: J. Robert Oppenheimer (left) of the 'Manhattan Project' with David Lilienthal, former President of the Atomic Energy Commission. Far right below: 'Little Boy', the uranium bomb.

. . . it's nearly level with me and climbing'. The giant cloud climbed on, 10,000 metres into the sky above the devastated city.

The local time was 08.16, when large numbers of Hiroshima's inhabitants were out in the streets, going to work or opening up their shops. As the fireball hit, thousands at its centre were vaporized by the intense heat; no trace of them was ever found. They were perhaps luckier than those just outside the central area, who were so badly burned that it was impossible to tell whether they were male or female. Over a 3.2 km (2 mile) radius houses made of wood, in the traditional Japanese style, burst into flames, roasting the inhabitants alive. Concrete buildings collapsed into piles of rubble, crushing people or imprisoning them so that they could only wait helplessly for the fires to reach them.

More than 80 per cent of the city's buildings were demolished, something like 68,000 in all. Most of those which remained standing, though battered, had been constructed to withstand earthquakes and had provided some protection for those inside. Survivors reported seeing the river clogged with corpses and, where walls were still standing, the shadows of people who had been near them at the time of the great flash, and whose images were left behind, like a primitive photographic negative. Occasionally a naked figure would appear, like something out of a nightmare, clothes burned off and skin hanging off in strips. For most people, there was no help available. The fire station was completely demolished, most of the city's medical staff were dead or injured and stores of medicines were destroyed. Rubble and earth alike were scorched to a reddish-brown and, a couple of hours after the explosion, there were sporadic showers of greasy black rain – water vapour mixed with radioactive dust, caused when carbon particles thrown up by the heat rose into a layer of cold air.

President Truman issued a new ultimatum to Japan to surrender but when there was no immediate response, the second bomb, 'Fat Boy', was dropped on Nagasaki, chosen because the original target, Kokura, was obscured by cloud. More than 24,000 people died. Still some of the Japanese army chiefs resisted the idea of unconditional surrender, determined to protect the position of the emperor, who was regarded as a divine ruler. It took the personal intervention of Emperor Hirohito, who summoned every member of the government to his presence and persuaded them to admit defeat, to bring the war to an end. Japan surrendered to the Allies on 14 August 1945.

By then, many of those in Hiroshima who had not been injured in the explosion were dying. They lost their appetites, developed persistent diarrhoea, their hair fell out and they started bleeding from the ears, nose and mouth. Even some of those who came to the city to help, a fortnight after the bombing, were affected by radiation sickness. By the end of 1945, 140,000 people had died in Hiroshima, and within five years another 60,000 had perished as a direct result of the events of 6 August. Even now, it is impossible to ascertain the full toll of death and injury. The long-term effects of radiation are still under scrutiny; it can cause cancers such as leukaemia, and possible birth defects in future generations. A study on the children of first generation victims at Yamaguchi University showed that one in four had birth defects. No one yet knows how many generations will be affected.

Below: The ravaged city of Hiroshima after the bomb, viewed from the roof of the Red Cross Hospital. Right: The horribly burned victims of the atom bomb. For most, there was little or no help available.

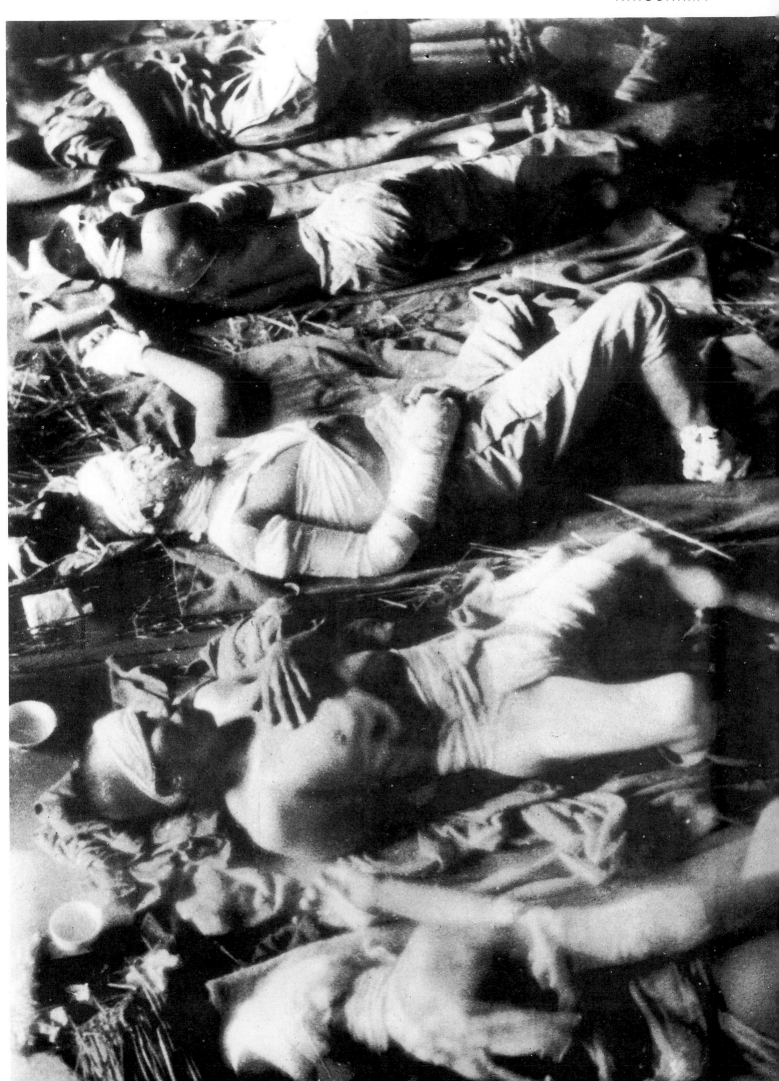

The Biafran Famine 1967-70

Reporters who flew into Biafra to report the war in 1968 were horrified to see the lines of starving children, their bodies wasted and their eyes dull.

After Nigerian independence in 1960, tensions built up between the Ibos, who came originally from the east, where there had been widespread conversion to Christianity, many of whom were now running successful businesses in other parts of the country and the northerners who greatly outnumbered them and therefore had more seats in the legislature. Power struggles led to violence and thousands of Ibo refugees fled to the east. In mid-1967 the military governor of the area, Colonel Emeka Ojukwu, announced that eastern Nigeria was to secede from the federation and become the independent state of Biafra. Within a month, civil war was declared, and it seemed to the outside world that the conflict would be brief, with Biafra quickly overwhelmed by the enormous strength of the federal army. However, the Biafrans proved stubborn, brave and ingenious. For 18 months they fought on, in spite of the blockade imposed by Nigeria, which stopped the import of normal food supplies.

As the army advanced gradually, the Ibos lost more and more of their most productive farmland and were squeezed into an ever-diminishing area. Villagers who had

Reporters who flew into Biafra to report the war in 1968 were horrified to see the lines of starving children, their bodies wasted and their eyes dull.

lived simply but had always had enough to eat now found themselves going hungry. The Biafrans showed great enterprise in finding ways round the blockade, with Catholic missionaries turned relief workers playing a major role; working from São Tomé, an island off the Nigerian coast, they flew in plane loads of dried fish. Their efforts were so successful that, at one time, the angry Nigerian government threatened to expel all Roman Catholic missionaries from its territory, but the missionaries could not hope to feed all the 8,000,000 people who, by early 1968, were surrounded by the federal army. Many had fled from their homes, leaving behind all their possessions. They were living in makeshift camps – and they were starving.

In the man-made famine of Biafra, more than 1,000,000 died of starvation, many of them children. Until the summer of 1968, the western media had paid little attention to the war in Biafra. Their governments supported Nigeria against the rebels, and readers had little interest in the conflict. However, in June a small party of British journalists flew in to report the progress of the war. What they found came as a tremendous shock; the emaciated bodies of the famine victims, the swollen bellies of the children, the shrunken faces of the babies. When they wrote that they had seen hundreds of children who would

have died of starvation by the time the report appeared in print and that Biafra was turning into another Belsen, world attention was suddenly focused on the plight of the break-away state.

Support for Biafra spread rapidly. In Britain, thousands demonstrated against a government that supported Nigeria. In Holland and Belgium Biafran supporters, backed by the Roman Catholic Church, forced a change in policy towards arms for Nigeria. In the United States, Senator Edward Kennedy, Chairman of the Senate Sub-Committee on Refugees, led a movement to change the government stance on Biafra. A vast international relief operation organized 40 flights of provisions a night.

However, it was obvious to all that Biafra could not hold out indefinitely against overwhelming odds. In early 1970

Biafrans who fled before the advancing federal army, leaving all their possessions behind, lived in makeshift refugee camps where there was never enough food to go round. Many died of starvation.

Colonel Ojukwu fled, and Biafra surrendered. Though the Nigerian government was skilful in its re-integration of the Biafrans, there was a bitter aftermath. The government halted all relief supplies from areas which had been aiding Biafra, and many observers believe that several thousand more lives were lost unnecessarily as the Biafrans waited for urgent food supplies to arrive on the slow route through Lagos, when airlifts from São Tomé or Gabon could have saved them.

Pol Pot in Cambodia 1975-79

The full horror of Pol Pot's tyrannical rule in Cambodia was only revealed when his régime was overthrown by the Vietnamese invasion of 1979. In four years he had virtually destroyed a nation, murdering 3,000,000 people as he tried to impose his fanatical will. The theory behind his Khmer Rouge party was that the country must go back to a primitive egalitarianism, a peasant economy with none of the trappings of modern industrial society.

When he took power after the overthrow of President Lon Nol, one of his first actions was to empty the capital, Phnom Penh, confiscating all possessions from its citizens and herding them into huge rural communes of as many as 10,000. The same evacuation took place in every town and even villages. Four years later, when refugees tried to return to their homes, they found that the buildings had been razed and, often, it was impossible to identify even the site of their villages.

Everyone from the age of seven was forced to work in the fields, including the pregnant, crippled, sick and dying. Those who collapsed and were unable to continue working were murdered where they lay. The new 'peasants' lived in malaria-ridden swamps without adequate food or shelter. They worked 9 days out of every 10, for 12 hours a day, existing on a daily ration of one bowl of gruel and a small piece of fish. Discipline was so strict that anyone eating fruit from a tree or catching crabs from a pool was sentenced to death.

Schools and colleges were abolished and all books were burned. The only type of education allowed was political indoctrination. Anyone with an education was an enemy of the state and must be eliminated; those who survived did so by concealing their intelligence. Thousands of others were executed along with the intellectuals: priests, all those associated with Lon Nol's rule, 'undesirables' like prison inmates and anyone who dared to question the system. Their mass graves were uncovered after the Vietnamese invasion. Their hands were still tied behind their backs and many had been blindfolded as they knelt on the edge of pits, waiting to be clubbed to death. The former Phnom Penh high school was turned into a prison and interrogation centre, and out of 16,000 'enemies' brought here, only five were known to have come out alive. Many of those tortured and killed were the wives and children of arrested men: reports of their suffering were used to persuade the victims to sign long confessions full of unlikely crimes.

Refugees who escaped with their lives told horror stories that the outside world found difficult to believe. The United States, war-weary and still smarting from its experiences in the Vietnam conflict, was reluctant to become involved in what might look like propaganda. In 1978, when Britain reported the régime to the United Nations Commission on Human Rights, the Commission could only agree to pass the allegations to the government in Phnom Penh for comment; the result was a hostile tirade against 'British imperialists'.

Despite the terrible legacy of Pol Pot, the Khmer Rouge continued to represent Cambodia at the United Nations while the new government, established after the Vietnamese invasion, was isolated by the international community and regarded as the puppet of Hanoi. Even now there are fears that, with the Vietnamese withdrawal, Pol Pot could win power again.

Below: A torture bed used by the Khmer Rouge at their interrogation centre in Phnom Penh, showing the manacles. Right: Bones and skulls from the 'killing fields', gruesome reminders of Pol Pot's murderous rule.

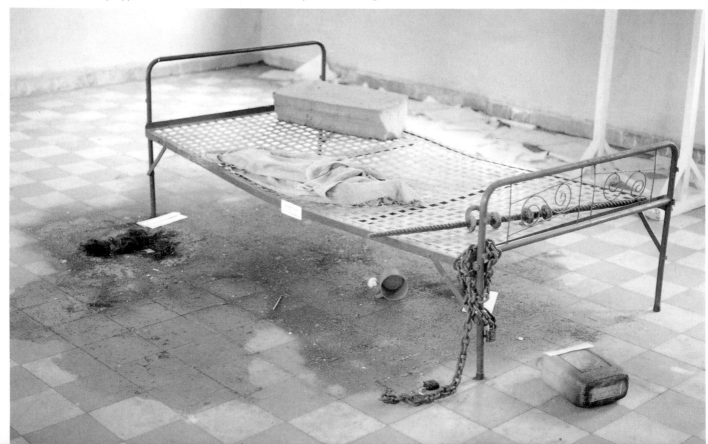

The Beirut Bombings 1983

There was a time when Beirut was known as the Paris of the Middle East, a playground for the wealthy, but by the time the multi-national peacekeeping forces arrived in the autumn of 1982, the city had been reduced to a ruined shell. Opposing Muslim and Christian factions fought for supremacy on the streets, and Israel had bombed the city to rout the Palestine Liberation Organization who used the Lebanon as a base for hostilities. When the American-organized peacekeeping force arrived, it brought hope of stability to tens of thousands of Lebanese. President Reagan announced that American Marines would stay until all Syrian and Israeli troops had withdrawn from Beirut.

The American forces might have seen themselves as peacekeepers but, to the extreme Muslim groups, their presence was further provocation. On 18 April 1983 a suicide bomber drove a van packed with explosives into the US Embassy. The seven-storey central section of the Embassy collapsed in dust and flames; bodies were flung 15 m (50 ft) into the air, so that they landed in the piles of glass and rubble in the street. Sixty people died and over 100 were injured, among them senior embassy staff, American marines and Lebanese civilians who were queuing in the ground floor visa section. American Ambassador Robert Dillon had been preparing to go out jogging when his office collapsed around him, but he suffered only cuts and bruises. The Islamic Jehad Organisation, a pro-Iranian group of Shiite Muslims, claimed credit for the attack.

Left: Beirut has suffered more than its share of conflict in recent years. Below: at the American base, tons of concrete was brought down when a suicide truck containing explosives drove into the building.

Worse was to follow. The level of violence escalated through the summer with heavily-armed factions battling through the ruins of burned-out buildings. Druze militiamen shelled Christian and Lebanese army positions from the hills above the city. In September a ceasefire seemed to promise some respite but the festering resentment of the continued presence of the 'peacekeepers' showed on 23 October, when there were simultaneous attacks on American and French headquarters in Beirut. The American Marine headquarters suffered most casualties when a Mercedes truck containing 2,270 kg (5,000 lb) of explosive crashed through the south gate, mowed down the guardhouse and ploughed on into the lobby of the building. It brought down hundreds of tons of concrete, burying dozens of soldiers, and high-rise buildings all over the city shook with the blast. Eyewitnesses reported that the road outside was like a slaughterhouse, littered with parts of human bodies and swimming with their blood. Two hundred and sixty men died – the greatest loss of life for American forces since the Vietnam War. Two minutes

after the attack, another truck full of explosives rammed into the French headquarters, 6 km (4 miles) away in the suburbs, killing more than 58 people.

Immediately after the attack, President Reagan insisted that the United States would not be intimidated by terrorists and that the continued presence of the Marines in Beirut was 'central to our credibility on a global scale'. However, political pressure was to force the President to end the USA's commitment to the multi-national force on 27 February 1984, after British and Italian forces had been withdrawn earlier in the month. In Beirut, the military and political situation deteriorated and the civil war raged on, with the taking of foreign nations as hostages becoming commonplace.

Below: Troops fight to extinguish the flames after the terrorist attack. Right: Young men carry their dead comrades from the ruined building. The attack on the French and American headquarters led subsequently to the withdrawal of American forces.

The Peking Massacre 1989

A harsh reminder that the process of political reform in Communist countries is by no means guaranteed came in June 1989 when troops and tanks ruthlessly crushed a student pro-democracy protest, killing as many as 1,000 and injuring at least as many more. For six weeks students, frustrated by the lack of progress towards reform, had occupied Tiananmen Square (the 'Gate of Heavenly Peace'), erecting barricades and building the 'Goddess of Democracy', a replica of the Statue of Liberty. About 150,000 troops had been stationed near the square since 20 May when the puppet Prime Minister Li Peng declared martial law, but there was enormous public support for the protesters and the government had repeatedly promised that force would not be used.

The first indication of the government's exasperation came on Saturday, 3 June when 10,000 soldiers from the Chinese People's Liberation Army, armed with clubs and knives, tried to clear the square. The confrontation ended in a humiliating defeat for the soldiers, who were driven back by hoards of protesters, chanting triumphant slogans.

Below: Thousands of students and other supporters of democracy, impatient for political reforms, gathered round a replica of the statue of liberty, called the 'Goddess of democracy', in Tiananmen Square.

Their triumph was to be short-lived. In the early hours of Sunday morning, soldiers poured into the square from the Great Hall of Peace while armoured personnel carriers moved in, crushing students as they lay in their tents. Tanks smashed through the barricades, volleys of machine-gun fire sprayed the side roads where thousands of people had gathered. Many protesters were shot in the back as they tried to flee; many uninvolved citizens died as they stepped out onto their doorsteps to see what was happening. Throughout the chaos, calm voices could be heard over official loudspeakers announcing that martial law must be imposed to protect 'the safety of the capital, the constitution and the socialist motherland'.

For seven hours the streets echoed with the sound of gunfire and the air was thick with the acrid smoke of tear gas. Protesters tried to resist by throwing petrol bombs, stones and bottles. Buses and trucks used as barricades went on blazing through the night. At the city hospitals, rows of injured people lay on blood-soaked mattresses on the floor, waiting for their wounds to be tended. The drivers of Peking's traditional tricycle carts braved bullets as they pedalled back and forth to the square collecting the wounded.

When the army moved in to oust the demonstrators from the square, hours of confrontation followed. The injured were ferried to hospital on bicycles and improvised stretchers.

As news of the bloodbath spread through Peking, the inhabitants were left in a state of horror and disbelief, appalled that the People's Army had fired on the people. Over the next couple of days the city was thrown into confusion. Most factories were on strike, most shops were closed, no public transport was available. As order was restored, the government issued a 'hit list' of wanted student leaders, those they labelled 'counter-revolutionary activists'. Many were arrested and produced at show trials where the verdict was never in doubt; some were even handed over by their own families.

Western governments, who had grown accustomed to thinking of China as a stable state making steady progress towards economic reform and modernization, were left in a state of shock by this evidence of savage repression. The massacre is likely to cost China dear in years to come, as in future foreign governments are unlikely to believe in further protestations of the government's benevolence.

Catastrophes of Nature

To a large extent, man's wellbeing depends on the stability and predictability of his natural environment, but there are times when nature runs riot – when a hurricane sweeps through a country like Honduras, demolishing all in its path or a river bursts its banks, turning towns and farmlands into a watery waste, or a virus rampages through society killing millions, like the Black Death in the 14th century or the flu epidemic of 1918-19.

A natural catastrophe may be swift and sudden, like a cyclone or a tornado, all over in minutes or hours or, like a flood, it may last for weeks or months. It may be slow and insidious, like drought, gradually tightening its grip and spreading its misery. Though prosperous countries are able to cushion themselves by storm warnings and sophisticated rescue services, not to mention insurance, countries of the Third World are desperately vulnerable to the vagaries of nature, with long-term hunger and privation following disasters like the Bangladesh floods of 1970 and the Ethiopian drought of the 1980s.

The Black Death 1346-50

From the beginning of 1346, rumours reached Europe of a strange and deadly plague that was killing thousands upon thousands in the East. Many who heard nodded comfortably and agreed that it was the punishment of God visited on the heathen. Then, within 18 months, it had reached the mainland of Europe, carried along with the exotic Eastern goods to the Italian ports, raging first through Italy, then France and Germany.

As it spread with alarming rapidity, many people left their homes, their families and all their possessions and fled to the country, thinking only of escaping from all contact with the sickness. Those who were brave enough to walk the streets often died there; whole families died shut away in their homes and only the smell of their rotting corpses prompted their neighbours to drag out the bodies, which were then carried away on carts, often stacked five or six high. When no consecrated ground was left for burial, bodies were stacked in pits. Boccaccio, writing about the effects of the plague in Florence, said 'Between March and the ensuing July, upwards of a hundred thousand human beings lost their lives . . . How many grand palaces, how many stately houses . . . once full of retainers, of lords, of ladies, were now left desolate of all, even to the meanest servant.'

In 1348, a ship brought the sickness to the Dorset coast of England. Over the year of 1349, so many people died that villages were left deserted and towns had too few inhabitants left to bury the dead. Geoffrey le Baker wrote: 'The pestilence seized especially the young and strong, commonly sparing the elderly and feeble. Scarcely anyone ventured to touch the sick and healthy persons shunned the . . . precious possessions of the dead, as infectious. People perfectly well on one day were found dead on the next.' As many as 2,500,000 people died in England; London alone lost 30,000 of its 70,000 population.

Medical knowledge was almost non-existent in the Middle Ages and so-called cures were closely bound up with superstitious ritual. In the face of the plague, the doctors were helpless. The idea that the cause lay in God's wrath with the wickedness of the suffering cities was deep-rooted. In some European cities, desperate inhabitants turned on the Jews, convinced that it was their fault for rejecting the reality of Christianity, and scores were burned at the scaffold. Churchmen issued calls to repentance and bands of flagellants appeared in the streets of European cities clad in sackcloth and ashes, their feet bare, scourging themselves with thongs until the blood ran, their purpose to atone for the sins of man and thus halt the plague. There was horror and bewilderment as it became obvious that the plague struck down everyone, righteous and unrighteous alike; in fact monasteries,

Groups of flagellants appeared in European towns, scourging themselves with whips, to atone for the sins they believed had caused the sickness.

where the monks lived in close proximity, were badly hit, sometimes leaving religious communities with only two or three monks and no one to lead them.

No one realized that the Black Death was spread by rat fleas, so no attempt was made to control the rats infesting trade ships or the insanitary medieval cities. The commonest form of sickness was the bubonic plague, which inflicted sufferers with 'bubos', painfully inflamed swellings in the groin or armpit, in addition to high fever, vomit-ing and delirium. The lucky few might survive the bubonic plague but there was a deadlier pneumonic version, where victims developed pneumonia and died very quickly. By 1350, somewhere between a quarter and a third of Europe's population had fallen victim to the Black Death.

The plague came like a demon of death from the skies, striking down the good and the bad indiscriminately, as this symbolic drawing shows.

Famine in Ireland 1846-49

In the 1840s the staple diet of the Irish peasants was the potato. It was the one crop that was prolific enough to feed a family all year round from a very small plot of land. The effects of any failure of the potato crop were catastrophic, as the 2,000,000 who depended on them could afford no other type of food, but in the summer of 1845 no one could have imagined what lay ahead. The early summer was fine and warm, then came plentiful rain in August and the crop looked splendid. Then, quite suddenly, reports of blighted potatoes, blackened and decayed, came from all over the country.

The cause was a parasitic fungus which had flourished in the wet weather, causing flourishing crops to wither within a few days. Even if the potatoes looked sound as

As starvation spread, the desperate Irish banded together to attack potato stores in their search for food, as in these riots reported in Galway.

they were dug, they gave off an unbearable stench when they were boiled and proved uneatable. Within six months, three quarters of Ireland's potato crop had been destroyed.

In 1846 the crop failed completely. The workhouses were full to overflowing and people were driven to eating nettles, roots and grass. So many died from starvation that there were not enough coffins and the bodies were buried tied up in straw; those who remained had 'more the appearance of ghosts than living beings'. A typhus epidemic raged through the country, often spread by those who fled from the worst-hit counties in the west.

The British government was slow to react and their measures fell far short of what was needed. Soup kitchens were set up, but they could only cater for a fraction of the needy. Programmes of public relief works were organized and, by spring 1847, they employed nearly 750,000 people, but wages were only a few pence a day, not enough to feed a family. Through the winter hundreds died beaking stones on the roads, among them women and children; the weather had sapped the last of their strength. Some towns reported 100 to 150 deaths a day.

Since the beginning of the famine, a steady trickle of emigrants had been leaving for America and Canada; by 1847 the trickle had become a flood. Anyone who could scrape together the passage money, or beg it from rela-

tives abroad, piled into the emigrant boats. In many cases, landlords gave their tenants the minimum sum necessary, simply to get rid of them from their estates. Many vessels were totally unsuitable for the voyage; some sank without trace, others arrived, months later, with most of their human cargo dead or dying. More than 17,000 people succumbed to starvation and fever on the journey.

In North America, efforts were made at keeping immigrants in quarantine – on Grosse Island in the St Lawrence River in Canada and Staten Island off New York – but their numbers were overwhelming. Ship after ship arrived in Montreal, disgorging hundreds of sick and destitute Irish, many of whom died on the wharves. Immigrants passed as healthy in hurried inspections on Staten Island took the fever into New York, where 1,396 deaths from typhus were recorded in 1847. Among the 1,000,000 or so immigrants to North America was the grandfather of the world-famous industrialist Henry Ford, maker of the Ford motor car.

In the years between 1846 and 1849, when the famine was at its height, Ireland lost more than a quarter of her population through starvation, disease and emigration, and the privations of those years left behind a deep resentment and distrust of England.

When the potato crop failed completely, families were forced to scavenge for food in the hedgerows or enter the overcrowded workhouses to survive.

The Dust Bowl 1930s

The violent dust storms that swept the mid-western states of the USA in the mid-1930s were to inflict terrible damage on one of the world's chief corn-growing regions and cause enormous misery to farming families.

In the early 19th century the Great Plains of the midwest, and the states of Oklahoma, Arkansas and Texas, had been known as the Great American Desert and in most years rainfall was sparse. The first settlers had been ranchers, but after the Homestead Act of 1862, which granted free homesteads of 65 ha (160 acres) to settlers who occupied the land for five years, the farmers poured in, ploughing up the natural grasslands of the Plains and planting wheat and corn. By the early 1900s, the population had increased tenfold and the harvests flourished in the years when rainfall was kind, so that by the 1920s this area had earned the name of the 'breadbasket of America'.

Then, in the next decade, came heatwaves and drought. Temperatures soared to 49°C (120°F) and hundreds of millions of dollars were lost in ruined crops. Strong winds raked at the unprotected soil, creating swirling dust storms which brought everything to a standstill: shops and schools closed, traffic came to a halt and even breathing became a problem. In the years 1933-5 the terrible 'black dusters' became part of life. A bad storm could send topsoil whirling 8 km (5 miles) into the air so that daytime was as dark as night and many saw it as a direct demonstration of the wrath of God. The storm of March 1935 blew without ceasing for 27 days and nights. Roads disappeared, farmhouses were buried up to their windowsills and roofs collapsed under the weight of soil deposited on them. Dust drifted as far as New England, where it caused blizzards of grey-black snow on the eastern coast.

Homesteaders who lost their land became seasonal farm labourers, living in squalid conditions and taking low paid work wherever it was offered.

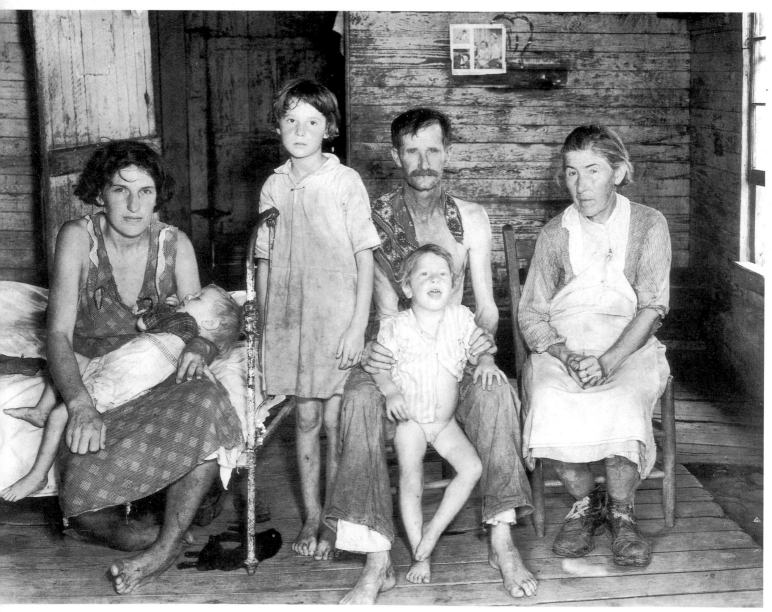

The terrible dust storms were fast and furious; this storm in the Pan handle was said to reach an amazing 145 kilometers (90 miles) per hour.

Worst hit were North and South Dakota, Nebraska, Kansas, Oklahoma, Minnesota, Iowa, Missouri, Montana, Wyoming, Colorado, Texas and New Mexico. Rivers dried up, livestock perished by the thousand, the former wheat and corn fields became an arid desert. Families could do nothing but watch their livelihoods destroyed. One story was told again and again about a Kansas farmer who went to the bank in the nearest town to try to raise a loan on his farm. The bank manager was explaining that he would have to come and inspect the farm before he made a decision when the farmer, seeing a dense black cloud rolling towards them, said: 'You don't have to bother. Here it comes now.'

These were the Depression years, when the whole country was suffering hardship and aid was severely limited. Many families had no choice but to load their possessions into trucks, leave their farms to the winds and make for California and a subsistence level existence as

day labourers. John Steinbeck graphically described their plight in his novel *The Grapes of Wrath*. Some 70,000 refugees fled the dustbowl states, leaving some areas with only 40 per cent of their previous population and 8 out of 10 of the remaining families on relief.

It was 1941 before the weather pattern returned to normal. Agricultural experts judged that one of the chief reasons for the wholesale disaster was that the land of the Great Plains had been over-ploughed and that half of it should be returned to pasture. Trees were planted as a brake on windblown soil and with new methods of irrigation and ploughing, the area became once more the greatest of the world's wheatbelts.

The Flu Epidemic 1918-19

As World War I was drawing to a close in the autumn of 1918 and the participants were counting the cost in terms of lives and economic damage, a new killer menace was tightening its grip all around the world, ravaging more families than the battles of the war. It was a virulent flu virus, spreading like wildfire. Some of those who caught it recovered; many did not. Complications frequently set in, the sufferer's lungs filled with fluid and severe pneumonia often followed. The disease fully earned its nickname of the 'lung plague'.

At the time it was reported that the disease had originated in Spain, but later it appeared that Spain was simply the first country to acknowledge it officially. In fact, the flu had already been spreading rapidly in the United States during the early part of the year and by March it had taken a grip in China. One popular theory was that it originated in the trenches and was brought back and spread by returning soldiers. Among British troops it was known as 'Flanders gripe'. Certainly the large number of troops being transported round Europe helped to spread the disease; crowded troop trains were hotbeds of contagion, and as soon as the soldiers arrived at their destinations, they passed on the flu to the local population. When the ship *Niagara* docked in Auckland, no quarantine regulations were imposed, and New Zealanders paid a high price for the laxity of the authorities with a total of 60,000 deaths throughout the country.

Some victims dropped dead in the streets and passers-by, fearing infection, walked into the roadway to avoid them. In many cities, cars ran into one another in the roads because the drivers were too ill to steer properly. Two ships in an Allied convoy off the coast of Ireland collided because everyone on board was affected by the virus and not a single member of the crew remained capable of steering a straight course.

In many countries cinemas and restaurants in the cities were closed, and offices staggered working hours in an effort to reduce the spread of infection. US police were issued with masks and street signs read 'It is unlawful to cough or sneeze. $500 fine'. In most countries, medical resources were stretched to breaking point. All attempts to find an effective 'flu vaccine failed and people were thrown back on their own remedies. There were reports of victims curing themselves by drinking several bottles of gin at a sitting, smearing hot bacon fat over their necks and chests or sitting all day surrounded by bowls of steaming eucalyptus oil. Some immersed themselves in near-boiling water, others lay in baths of ice. New Orleans residents plastered their skin with vinegar several times a day. The violent nosebleeds that sometimes accompanied the disease could be a blessing; regular bleeding seemed to get rid of the infection.

By January 1919, the epidemic had run its course. A report by the International Commission on Hygiene estimated that 50 per cent of the world's population had succumbed in some degree and more than 20,000,000 had died – more than those killed in the whole of World War I. In Asia, nearly 16,000,000 died, in Europe over 2,000,000 and in North and South America, around 1,400,000. It was the worst epidemic since the Black Death and, like the plague before it, it seemed to pass by the weak and sickly and pick on the strong and fit: 85 per cent of the deaths were in the 17-40 age group.

As the epidemic spread over the world, people came up with their own ways of avoiding infection. These flu masks were pictured on the streets of Paris.

Floods

China's Yellow River

Over the 4000 years of its history, China's Yellow River has caused more death and destruction than any other natural feature in the world and it fully deserves its nickname as 'China's Sorrow'. Its colour comes from the enormous quantities of yellowish silt that the river carries on its 4,500 km (2,800 mile) journey from the border of Tibet to the Yellow Sea. As the river meanders through the Great Plain of northern China it deposits layers of silt along its way so that the bed rises and in many places the river runs 4.5 m (15 ft) above the fertile flat lands.

The Chinese have been battling with the menace of the Yellow River since the beginning of recorded time. Ancient legend tells of a 13-year flood 4,300 years ago, which would have submerged the country for ever if the Emperor had not chosen Yu, the 'Son of Heaven', to bring the raging waters under control. His success was such that the river remained quiet for the next 1,500 years. Yu was created Emperor and is still revered as 'Yu the Great'.

The first set of levees were built in 602 BC and since then millions of workers have toiled to build up the protective dykes. Yet, in spite of all efforts to restrain it, the Yellow River has breached restraints something like 1,500 times over the centuries and the farmers who eked out a perilous existence on the fertile lands of the plains grew used to hardship. As the population increased more lives were at risk from each successive innundation and the nightmare floods of 1887 took a grim toll of human life.

It was late September that year that the river, swollen by heavy rains, broke through the dykes at a sharp bend near Chengchou, about 64 km (40 miles) from Kaifong in the heavily populated province of Honan. It tore a gap of 90 m (300 ft), rapidly widening until it measured nearly 1 km and the waters poured unchecked onto the Great Plain. At its height the flood covered 480 km (300 miles), covering 11 cities and 1,500 villages. Night after night the darkness was filled by the weeping and calling of the helpless and injured. Small boats braved the still churning water, throwing bread to marooned victims with no immediate hope of rescue. The *North China Herald* reported that straw ricks whirled along in the water 'each with its weeping load of men and women. In one place a dead child floated to shore on the top of a chest where it had been placed for safety by its parents, with food and name attached. In another place a family, all dead, were found with the child placed on the highest spot on a couch, well covered by clothes.'

The waters themselves killed 900,000 people, though as many again succumbed to the disease and starvation that followed and uncounted millions were homeless. It was over 18 months before the army of workers could seal the breaches and control the river once more, so that some semblance of normal life could begin again. Even after that the floods remained an almost yearly hazard, capable of claiming thousands of lives until in 1947 huge dynamiting operations returned the river to its former path and the 1950s brought an enormous water management programme of rivers and dams which have lessened the danger without removing it.

China's Yellow River can kill many thousands of people when flood waters pour over the Great Plain.

The Mighty Mississippi

The Mississippi is America's most important river, running for 6,100 km (3,800) miles from its beginning in a pine-fringed lake in northern Minnesota to the Gulf of Mexico, fed by as many as 100,000 rivers and streams, including the Missouri, Ohio, Arkansas and Illinois. The waters have always held hidden menace and some experts believe that floods pose a greater threat to both people and property than the notorious San Andreas fault.

In the early 18th century, French settlers in Louisiana began a system of earthen levees or dykes to hold back the Mississippi's frequent floods. These were raised and strengthened over the years until at the turn of the 20th century they extended for hundreds of kilometres on either side of the river, under the supervision of the Mississippi River Commission. They were frequently breached but, after major expenditure following the flood of 1922, the Commission claimed that the levee system was now 'in condition to prevent the disastrous effects of floods.'

In April 1927 they were proved appallingly wrong. After an autumn and winter of heavy rain the tributaries of the Mississippi swelled, joining together to form a huge rolling tidal wave which was to break through the levees in 120 places. At one spot, where the break was 1.5 km (1 mile) wide, an eyewitness said that the water rushed through as a 'tan-coloured wall 2 m (7 ft) high and with a roar as of a mighty wind.' The houses of 750,000 people disappeared below the waters and millions of acres of land through seven states was inundated. Cairo, Illinois, was flooded to a depth of 17 m (56 ft) and 3 m (10 ft) of water stood in the business district of Montpelier, Vermont. Water poured into Arkansas at such a rate that mules in harness, pulling waggons about their normal business at noon, had been drowned where they stood. Near the mouth of the Arkansas River several hundred people trying to reach safety were stranded on a long steel bridge across the river for three days and three nights before rescue boats could reach them.

New Orleans was only saved by blasting a gap in the levee below the city so that the floodwaters could reach the sea via a short cut across the land, rather than following the course of the river; the dynamiting went ahead in spite of the protests of those whose homes lay in its path.

The great brown sea of the flood did not recede until July. Red Cross centres were set up to care for 350,000 refugees with nowhere to go. Over 300 people had been killed, some of them swept away as they tried in vain to sandbag the leaks in the levees. The damage was estimated at $300 million.

Following the events of 1927, a whole new system of flood control was built, including vast storage reservoirs, and spillways into new channels. Flood control may have helped to limit damage but the Mississippi remains untamed. There was a major flood in 1937 when 13,000 homes were destroyed and in 1973, 69,000 people lost their property. In 1983 the swollen waters caused $450 million of damage and there may be far more trouble in store. A recent study by Louisiana State University showed that the volume of the Mississippi has risen by 250 per cent over the past 50 years.

When the mighty Mississippi bursts through the system of levees, farmlands disappear beneath the water, homes are flooded and livestock drowned.
Inset above: Chain gangs were used to work on the vital levees when floods were approaching; this prisoner is taking a rest from his labours.

Florence Under Water 1966

In the 16th century Leonardo da Vinci devised plans for controlling the river Arno so that Florence would no longer be menaced by flood. His scheme was never adopted and, though major floods were recorded every 26 years or so, the city remained unprepared for the catastrophe of 1966 when over one third of the city's annual rainfall came down within 48 hours. High winds and heavy rains pounded the whole of Italy in early November, causing extensive floods in the north and central parts of the country. Then, on 4 November, the Arno, which runs through the older section of the city, burst its banks, turning into a seething torrent and spreading ever wider, its waters thick and sticky with hundreds of tons of silt washed down from the hills. Oil from burst furnaces and storage tanks mixed with the river water, adding its own destructive power.

In places the waters rose to 4.5 m (15 feet); they swamped magnificent buildings like the 13th century church of Santa Croce, the Medici Chapel, the San Firenzi Palace and the Casa di Dante. At the Baptistry in the Piazza del Duomo five of Ghiberti's bronze panels of biblical scenes were ripped from the doors. Most Florentines could only concentrate on getting to safety as fast as possible, but at the Institute of the History of Science the director clambered along a third floor ledge to the Uffizi Gallery next door thirty times, rescuing dozens of irreplaceable works of art. Tens of thousands of people clung to the roofs of their homes throughout the night, dreading the rise of the swirling black water below. By morning the weather was dry and bright and the flood began to recede, leaving behind a thick layer of stinking mud and slime.

Mercifully the final death toll was only 35 but the cultural catastrophe in this cradle of the Italian Renaissance, where many of the world's greatest art treasures were stored, caught the imagination of the world. The city had been so ill-prepared for the crisis that many great masterpieces were stored in vulnerable basements. Below the Uffizi Gallery 600 old master paintings were submerged in oily water for hours and 130,000 photographic negatives of Florentine art were completely ruined.

There were other major losses: the Etruscan collections from the Archaeological Museum, the musical scores of Scarlatti, the private papers of Amerigo Vespucci, the Italian explorer who gave his name to America, were all damaged beyond repair. The monks of Santa Croce worked knee deep in mud to rescue the 700-year-old *Crucifixion* by Cimabue, but though experts were to work for ten years on its restoration, the painting was largely destroyed.

Helpers flocked in from all over Europe and America, including the foremost experts in Renaissance art and specialists in restoration work. Hundreds of volunteers worked to recover 6,000,000 valuable volumes lying underwater

When the flood waters subsided, the square before the Basilica of Santa Croce was a sea of mud.

at the Biblioteca Nazionale and the State Archives, many wearing gas masks to keep from choking on the foul smell. Many of the books had become like blocks, solidified by the melted glue of their bindings. They were dried out in tobacco sheds and textile plants, then each one had to be painstakingly restored, treated with chemicals and every page gently prised away from its neighbour. Ghiberti's magnificent bronze panels were rescued and replaced and the 500-year-old wood sculpture of Mary Magdalene by Donatello recovered surprisingly well from its watery ordeal.

Within a year the galleries and libraries were reopened with many of their treasures on show once more and Italy was able to claim that 'the golden city of the Renaissance glitters again.'

The floods caused an enormous amount of damage to works of art, like the *Crucifixion* in Santa Croce.

Storms

The Long Island and New England Hurricane 1938

The storm of 21 September 1938 cut a terrifying path of destruction 523 km (325 miles) long, right along the eastern seaboard of the USA, from the beaches of Long Island up to Montreal. Hurricane force winds, some of the highest ever recorded on the North American continent, screamed all the way from New York to Boston and great menacing waves smashed over the coasts of Connecticut, Long Island and Rhode Island, killing over 600 and demolishing more than 60,000 buildings.

The storm caught forecasters unawares: the previous day they had closely monitored a storm that menaced Florida, and the inhabitants, accustomed to taking precautions to protect themselves and their property, were on the alert. However, the hurricane had changed course and seemed to be heading harmlessly away. But instead of dissipating over the ocean as expected, it gathered speed and headed north, straight for New England.

As the wind whipped up the sea off the coast of Long Island, the residents, unaware of the mayhem to come, phoned friends to come and see the great breakers pounding the shore. It was early afternoon when the wind came tearing in, ripping off roofs and tumbling cars. The inhabitants fled, so that when a 12 m (40 ft) wall of water hit the land, many were caught in the open and smashed to death on the wreckage. Others managed to scramble onto the roofs of their houses and clung there as the buildings were carried out to sea.

Telephone and telegraph wires came down and there was no chance to send out warnings before the storm hit Rhode Island, so suddenly that on one beach alone 41 people were drowned; only a few minutes earlier they had been paddling or enjoying picnics. One woman spent a whole night floating on a telegraph pole, buffeted this way and that by the waters of the Atlantic; the broken wires had wrapped tightly round her and she had been unable to break free. On one of the islands off the Connecticut coast a school bus was swept into the sea and only one child was saved.

As the powerful mass of water smashed into the bay at providence, Rhode Island, it carried the lighthouse away like a child's toy, and pounded hundreds of boats into kindling. When it rolled on into the downtown business district, it brought walls down onto automobiles as they stalled in the streets and then submerged them. As the waters rose, those lucky enough to be in high buildings let down ropes and sheets to haul up others marooned below. Many who had been working on ground level had to swim for their lives. Only the looters remained unafraid, plunging through the water to plunder the unprotected shops.

In New London, Connecticut, fire broke out on the waterfront and the high winds drove it hungrily from building to building. Even when fire engines managed to fight their way through the floods to reach the blaze, the winds blew the water back on the fire-fighters and for six hours the fire blazed unhindered. The eventual bill for damage came to $1 million.

When the storm had finally blown itself out, after rampaging through Montreal, Canada, it left harbours clogged with smashed boats, forests flattened, crops devastated, and roads blocked by houses which had been lifted bodily and thrown down again. At least 32,000 km (20,000 miles) of telephone and telegraph cables were down and wreckage littered the main railroad tracks, so that it was many weeks before the main line from New York to Boston could be re-opened.

The Honduras Hurricane 1974

Even before the terrible hurricane Fifi hit Honduras on 18 September 1974, the country was virtually a disaster area. This small country, lying on the Caribbean in the north and the Pacific on the west and south-west, and with Nicaragua to the east and Guatemala to the west, is the poorest in mainland Central America. The people are mostly of Indian stock, living in primitive conditions, where $250 a year is considered a good wage.

The death toll from hurricanes in the area has been so high that the United States and neighbouring countries have developed advanced meteorological services to monitor the atmospheric conditions that give rise to such storms. As hurricane Fifi gathered strength an urgent warning went to the Honduras government but the country's poor communications system meant that there was no chance of getting the news to the outlying areas and even those who knew of the danger could do little but wait and hope.

The hurricane arrived in the middle of the night, the winds flattening buildings in their path and the torrential rain that followed swelling the rivers until they overflowed into raging floods. The flimsy homes of farmers and peasants, built of stone, wattle and clay, disappeared or were carried off on the water, to be smashed to pieces on the river banks and other obstructions.

In the country's second city, San Pedro Sula, 400,000 people were left homeless and without food. One of the worst hit areas was the riverside district round Choloma where everything was swept away and 3,000 people (half the town's population) lost their lives. Many survivors had tragic tales to tell. One reported that people had been terrified to leave their homes: 'I saw nine people from one family embrace one another; they were afraid to move. They died, holding each other in their arms.' An old man whose whole family had been drowned in the flood went back to search the wreckage of his home to find several bodies of complete strangers, 'just poor innocents who were swept down from the mountain and ended up here'. As the floods receded, bodies lay everywhere, many half-buried in thick mud. The government became so worried about epidemics of cholera and typhoid that they ordered the mass burning of thousands of victims.

Bridges and railway tracks had been swept away and roads were buried in mud so, at first, helicopters from the United States base in the Panama Canal Zone were the only means of rescue. They hovered over the devastated areas where survivors clung desperately to anything that protruded from the swirling water, and hauled up wet and hungry people from roofs and tree-tops.

The entire crop of bananas and coffee, the most important exports, had been destroyed, together with subsistence crops like rice, corn and beans. Livestock had perished by the thousand. People who had been hungry before the disaster were quickly reduced to starvation. With the government unable to organize an effective relief programme, the population relied heavily on overseas help but aid workers had to struggle against flagrant corruption and inefficiency. Their suppliers were frequently diverted into the black market, and at first it was impossible for them to help the stricken areas. There were many stories of troops, who were supposed to help with distribution, fighting the Red Cross workers when they tried to stop them from plundering the medical supplies. Eventually corruption was brought under control and the serious work of rehabilitation began but it was an uphill struggle for a country in such dire economic need.

Right: In New Hampshire, the hurricane tore off the steeple of the Community Church at Dublin and upended it so that the point smashed down on the pew usually occupied by the minister's wife. Below: The Honduras hurricane flattened buildings in its path and left behind a muddy wasteland.

The Tornadoes of the American Midwest 1974

Many areas of the United States are only too familiar with the dangers of tornadoes; the inhabitants have learned where to take shelter when the warnings are given and in the worst areas, they can take refuge in their specially built storm cellars. However, the storms of 2-3 April 1974 ravaged areas unfamiliar with tornadoes. In eight hours, more than 100 tornadoes roared through an area from Alabama and Georgia to Windsor, Ontario, across the Canadian border, killing 324 people and injuring hundreds more. Two of the worst hit towns were Xenia, Ohio, and Brandenburg, Kentucky, neither of which had much experience of killer storms. Brandenburg had never experienced a tornado before and though there had been several in the Xenia area within living memory, they had never been fierce enough to cause loss of life.

Brandenburg was a quiet, slow-moving farming com-munity of 1,600 on the banks of the Ohio, west of Louis-ville. In just a few terrifying minutes, three quarters of the town's buildings were demolished; houses, cars and bodies were whirled through the air and smashed to the ground. Later, as the river was dragged for bodies and the death toll rose to 29, including a large number of children, many of the survivors collected what they could salvage and left for ever; so much had gone that rebuilding seemed impossible. The town of Brandenburg had died.

In Xenia, a twister smashed a 6.5 km (4 mile) path of destruction, making no distinction between old and new developments, demolishing churches, homes and shops alike. Within five minutes, 30 people were dead, nearly 100 injured and thousands were rendered homeless. Luckily the storm hit outside school hours, or far more lives would have been lost when the top floor of the high school was blown away and school buses were tossed into the auditorium.

In north-west Alabama, the little town of Guin was wiped off the map; 'Guin just isn't there,' reported a state trooper. A radio reporter at nearby Jasper told his listen-ers: 'We can't talk to the police department. It just blew

A tornado can be a terrifying sight; this tornado in Cincinnati, the worst in 49 years, is pictured just as it touches down to begin wreaking havoc.

away.' In Sugar Valley, Georgia, a nine-year-old boy was the sole survivor of a family of five. He was playing outside when the tornado picked him up and carried him for 180 m (200 yds) before dropping him to the ground; his mother, father and two sisters died in the wreckage of their home.

A state of emergency was declared and the national guard was ordered out in Ohio, Kentucky, Alabama, Indiana and Tennessee. Damage to personal property was estimated at hundreds of millions of dollars and low interest loans were granted to home-owners and business-men.

Tornadoes are some of nature's most violent and awesome storms; nothing can be done to prevent them, and little is known about them. Though hurricanes can be observed from within, the smaller size of the tornado makes this impossible. Research has shown that they originate within small cyclones, which in turn arise within large thunderstorms. Tornadoes approach with a scream-ing roar and, though their life span is usually less than 15 minutes, winds in the twister funnel can swirl at more than 480 km (300 miles) an hour, four times as fast as those of a hurricane. At the edge of the funnel, the force is still powerful enough to uproot trees; at the centre buildings are blown over. No one caught in the direct path of a tor-nado without suitable shelter has much chance of survival.

Tornado damage in this area of Kentucky, as well as in many other states, was so severe that a state of emergency was declared as clearing up began.

More Monster Storms

A devastating storm struck the busy port of Galveston, Texas, on 8 September 1900. The city, with its 40,000 inhabitants, was built along a narrow island with no protection from the fury of the weather. By the time anyone realized that a major hurricane was on its way it was too late to leave the island; the bridges were under water and communications with the mainland were severed.

There were few places to take shelter but 400 found safe refuge in the Sacred Heart Church, though the roof was torn off and part of the walls crumbled. They were among the lucky ones; 90 children were killed when their orphanage collapsed around them. More than 5,000 were injured, many seriously, and half of all the town's buildings were demolished.

So many hundreds of people had died that corpses lay in long rows on the floor of warehouses used as makeshift funeral parlours. Free bourbon was dispensed to volunteers who dug out body after body from the wreckage. The heat was too great to allow time for proper burials, so mass cremations were held.

By the time Hurricane Camille struck in 1969, meteorological techniques had improved, so that it was preceded by urgent warnings and a programme of evacuation. Even so, more than 200 people died as it swept across Mississippi and Louisiana, turning the two states into official disaster areas. Among those who had ignored the evacuation warnings were the occupants of a block of beachfront apartments in Pass Christian, Mississippi, who planned to hold a 'hurricane party' and enjoy the excitement. Out of 24 merry-makers, only one woman survived. As the tidal wave hit the building, she was washed out through a window, while the whole building crumbled behind her.

A sudden storm can often result in a flash flood when heavy rains are funnelled through a narrow space, causing local devastation – and reliable prediction is almost impossible. The violent thunderstorm over Willow Creek, Oregon on 14 June 1903, was all over in an hour but it killed more than 200, one third of the population of a single town. The holiday mood of campers in Big Thompson Canyon on a July Saturday in 1976 soon turned to terror as a violent thunderstorm brought down part of the mountainside and swept away everything in its path. Though Britain seldom has to face massive storms, the Devon town of Lynmouth was wrecked in the summer of 1952, when the East and West Lynn rivers turned into raging torrents, bringing hundreds of tons of boulders crashing through the centre of the town. Nearly 100 homes were smashed to pieces and 34 people lost their lives.

Right: While hurricane Camille raged, this 26 m (85 ft) boat was borne in on flood tides to be deposited in the yard of a home in Biloxi, Mississippi. Above right: The Galveston storm of 1900 flattened half the town's buildings into piles of timber.

However, the local effects of such a storm are eclipsed by the widespread devastation caused by a tropical cyclone, which develops at something like 100 times the energy of an atomic bomb. The winds themselves are terrifying but the worst destruction usually results from the tidal waves they whip up, or by the floods when rivers burst their banks. Japan has to face an average of four typhoons a year, so that the annual bill for the damage they cause runs into hundreds of millions. In 1953 a typhoon caused over 42,000 casualties in the city of Nagoya alone, nearly 2,000 of them dead or missing. In 1959, a fierce typhoon struck Honshu, causing nearly 4,500 deaths and leaving 1,500,000 million homeless.

Even these figures cannot compare with teh catastrophes which the angry elements can inflict on the Third World. Those living in prosperous countries can modify their buildings, build storm shelters beneath their homes and, if necessary, carry out expensive evacuations. Though the costs of hurricane damage in the United States have risen sharply over the past 50 years, the number of deaths have steadily declined. In Japan, after the port of Osaka had been swamped by tidal waves six times in 30 years, $560 million was spent on a massive typhoon defence system, which took 16 years to complete. In poor countries, where millions of people are on or below the breadline, in areas where transport facilities are almost non-existent, there is no chance of escape. Even when the coming storm is identified well in advance the majority of the luckless inhabitants have to stay put and hope that they will survive.

One of the worst cyclones ever recorded in the Indian Ocean struck in November 1977, when fierce winds tore down trees and swept aside buildings and a 20 ft (6 m) high tidal wave crashed into the province of Andhra Pradesh. Whole villages were wiped out and in some country districts 90 per cent of the population lost their lives. Reports from relief helicopters told of waterlogged landscape as far as the eye could see, with only the top of an occasional tree visible. The bloated carcasses of dead animals floated on the water, as well as human corpses. In spite of the efforts of relief workers to provide food to the survivors, many were to starve. More than 100,000 people died, even though the storm warnings were given 48 hours ahead.

When this century's fiercest cyclone hit one of the most densely populated regions of the world, the resulting human tragedy was horrifying in scale and in the long term, the political results were to be remarkable. On 10 November 1970, meterorologists identified a depression forming in the Bay of Bengal, rapidly turning into a cyclonic storm. Three days later hurricane force winds whipped up a great tidal wave which devastated the flat, low-lying land of East Pakistan, where 1,200 people were crowded into every square mile, people who were among the poorest in the world, scratching a bare living from the soil. The official death toll was 300,000 but outside observers calculated that it was nearer to 1,000,000. Reporters and rescue workers, moving into the area after the flood, found that in some villages it was impossible to walk without treading on the dead bodies covering the roads and every tree was festooned with bodies.

The misery and chaos that followed the storm was to turn to rebellion; much of the blame was laid at the door of the government of Pakistan, over 1,500 miles (2,400 km) away in the capital city of Karachi. Little money had been spent on flood control measures in the vulnerable area and the rescue services had been inadequate and slow in coming. The movement towards self-government gathered force and turned into civil war. Eventually the state of Bangladesh was born. Sadly, changes of government do not mean the end of the natural disasters of Bangladesh. The country is the most populous on earth, the land – fertile because it is so often submerged – is flat, with no natural barriers to hold back the sweeping flood water and even in the 1980s, the storms took a high toll in human life.

Below: After the Indian cyclone of 1977, the bodies of whole families floated in the murky waters. Right: Frequent floods in Bangladesh leave thousands of hungry refugees with no way of earning a living.

Drought

Memories of the dreaded Dust Bowl of the 1930s were stirred once more in the United States in 1976-77, when a prolonged drought hit the western and mid-west states. Reservoirs ran dry, crops failed and farmers went bankrupt. In the Pacific north-west, where the winter had brought none of the expected snow to fill rivers and lakes, hydroelectric power was in danger of shutdown. The economy of California was near ruin as crops dependent on constant irrigation died away for lack of water and farmers sold up and moved away. Losses were reckoned at $1 billion. In the Midwest, too, farmers faced dramatic losses. There was little food for cattle and prices went sky-high, so cattlemen were forced to slaughter livestock by the thousand or sell them for a pittance. Governors of eleven of the drought-hit states set up a special task force to co-ordinate drought relief but the crippling financial disaster could hardly have come at a worse time, when the government was already struggling with the worst economic conditions since World War II, and several Federal Aid projects to bring more water to arid regions had recently been cut.

Drought struck again in 1988, with areas in the Midwest and south declared disaster areas. Montana, North Dakota, Tennessee, Georgia and North Carolina had less than a quarter of their usual level of rainfall, causing waterways to dry up and turning pastures into arid plains. Dust storms scoured off topsoil from millions of acres of farmland and the level of the Mississippi fell so low that in places it became unnavigable.

When drought affects the developed world farmers may face bankruptcy but their families do not die of starvation. In the Third World the situation is tragically different. There, in a matter of months, a drought can push thousands across the thin line that separates constant hunger from starvation. At least 50,000,000 people, dependent on the precarious agriculture of the semi-desert regions of the world, are at risk of their lives when the rains fail. Though the tragedy of the Ethiopian famine burst on the world's headlines as a revelation in 1984, the problem was far from new. In the African Sahel belt – those countries bordering the southern Sahara – life is a constant struggle for survival. Even when Ethiopia is not stricken with famine, about 1,000 children die every day from the effects of malnutrition. Yet the population continues to rise, increasing competition for already inadequate supplies of food. According to the World Bank, the sub-Sah-

When drought strikes in the American midwest, crops are ruined and farmers face enormous losses.

aran population, numbering 385,000,000 in 1980, will have more than doubled by 2005.

The underlying causes of famine are far too complex to be blamed entirely on the weather. The desert encroaches by thousands of kilometres a year because of overgrazing and mistaken use of land. The poverty-stricken herdsmen of the Sahel belt are too cut off from central government to pressure them into action, and money sorely needed to feed the hungry is often diverted into arms spending. In some of the worst affected countries – Chad, Ethiopia, Angola, Mozambique and the Sudan – famine exists alongside wars and tribal conflicts that swallow up government resources and, as a final blow, often make it impossible for foreign aid to reach those in desperate need.

Even before the great famine, the people of Ethiopia were always hungry and children died every day from the terrible effects of malnutrition.

It is, however, drought that precipitates disaster. When rainfall had been well below average in the Sahel region during the five years up to 1972, the pattern of events was depressingly familiar. At first, as fodder became scarce, the herdsmen began selling their livestock but as supply exceeded demand, prices crashed and they were forced to slaughter their cattle. Once the meat and then the remaining grain was eaten, the people moved south in droves, swelling the already overcrowded cities in search of non-existent food. Numbers are almost impossible to gauge in this remote region, but it seems likely that 200,000 perished in Ethiopia alone between 1972 and 1974.

In theory, famine on this scale should no longer exist. The early warning system set up by the UN Food and Agriculture Organization is meant to monitor data about rainfall, planting and harvests so that a clear picture of abnormal shortages will emerge long before they turn to catastrophe. In practice, the system has to rely on information from individual governments and in many countries, data collection is woefully inadequate.

The rains failed in 1982, and in the two subsequent years, and by the end of 1984, 20 African countries were seeking emergency food aid. By then more than 5,000,000 infants were dying every year and over 150,000,000 people faced starvation. In Ethiopia, the country with the lowest average income in Africa, where the government had appealed for food aid every year for 11 years, the grip of famine quickly became a stranglehold. Though reports of the country's plight appeared in the western media several times during 1984, it was a BBC film, shot on location in northern Ethiopia that October, showing thousands of starving men, women and children waiting to die, that stirred the conscience of the world.

The film showed the towns of Makalle and Korem; they were, said the commentator, 'the closest thing to hell on earth'. Tens of thousands of refugees had converged on the towns from the drought-stricken areas. Some had walked 200 km (125 miles), leaving members of their family dead along the way. They squatted in the dirt, too weak to swat away the swarms of flies that surrounded them: their bodies wasted, their legs like matchsticks, they held babies with wizened faces like monkeys, too weak to move or cry. Relief workers, overwhelmed by the numbers, could only select a certain number for the distribution of the small amount of available food, knowing that they were condemning the rest to death.

The pictures were worse than anything western eyes had seen since the gates of the concentration camps were opened at the end of World War II, and the response was immediate and impressive. Contributions flooded in and performers staged a mammoth rock concert, Live Aid, organized by singer Bob Geldorf.

By May, 1985, up to 500,000 tons of food had been delivered but the international relief effort operated under great difficulties. Distribution was hampered by lack of transport and by continuing wars in Eritrea and Tigre. Relations between humanitarian agencies and government agencies were often strained, particularly over the huge resettlement programmes, where hundreds of thousands of people were moved – many, it was claimed, forcibly – to the more fertile regions of western and southern Ethiopia.

Once the rains returned in late 1985, refugees began to return to their homes and with outside help crops were planted, livestock replaced and village communities began to rebuild their lives. Then, in 1987, came news of further famine in Ethiopia when drought once again destroyed the main harvest of the north, while areas not affected by drought saw crops badly damaged by a plague of locusts. It was a shock reminder that the problems of sub-Saharan Africa will only be solved by long-term international effort.

Left: The conscience of the world was touched by the tragic pictures from Ethiopia. Below: Irish pop star Bob Geldof organized the brilliant Live Aid concert to raise money for the famine victims.

AIDS

Above: As part of the anti-AIDS campaign, posters warn of the dangers of drug users sharing needles. Right: The number of deaths from AIDS has been growing with alarming speed. Young Americans gather to view a quilt made in memory of their friends who have already died from the disease.

According to the World Health Organization, AIDS – acquired immune deficiency syndrome – is 'the worst public health disaster ever'. It was first recognized in 1981 and since then has developed at a frightening rate; somewhere between 5,000,000 and 10,000,000 people worldwide have been infected with the human immuno-deficiency virus (HIV), of whom 15,000 have already developed full-blown AIDS. In spite of an enormous international research programme, scientists are no nearer to finding a cure for the disease, which is spread through infected blood or body fluids.

In 1981 an apparently new disease was reported among homosexuals by the Centers for Disease Control in Atlanta, Georgia, in the United States. It was soon obvious that it was multiplying at an alarming rate. By 1984 there were 5,557 cases in the USA, by 1985 there were 9,581, and soon the number was doubling every 13 months or so. In 1982 there were just three cases in Britain but by 1985 there were 165.

Fear and mystery has surrounded the spread of the new killer disease and, as it seemed at first confined to the homosexual community, it was nicknamed the 'gay plague'. However, though homosexuals are still the highest risk group in the United States and Europe, followed by intravenous drug users sharing needles, in Africa – where 4,000,000 are thought to be infected – the spread has been mainly by heterosexual contact. At the time when scientists were first working to identify the disease in the United States, large numbers of heterosexuals in African countries were already dying of AIDS. In some urban centres in central Africa, one third of the population is believed to be infected with the virus.

Retrospective research indicates that HIV infection has existed in Africa since 1959, and some scientists believe that the virus came from green monkeys in Central Africa and has been transmitted to man through bites, mutating and becoming a killer. Other theories, never substantiated, have claimed that the virus was the by-product of cancer research in laboratories; that it was collected by American germ warfare experts in Africa for future military use; or that it was deliberately created by scientists as a weapon of destruction, then tested on prisoners who were released into the community later because no-one realized the length of the incubation period of the disease.

There have been calls for compulsory screening, for checks on all foreign visitors, for a register of those found to be HIV positive and even, in the United States, for quarantine camps for infected people. Up till now, western governments have relied for controlling AIDS on wide-scale advertising to put over the risks and the methods of avoiding infection. So far, the evidence is that only the homosexual community – like that of San Francisco, where nearly 90 per cent now use methods to eliminate infection – has taken the warnings to heart.

The epidemic is worsening all the time, with 122

countries now reporting cases of AIDS. The Centers for Disease Control forecasts that by 1991 the number of cases diagnosed in the United States during the year will rise to 74,000 and the number of deaths to 54,000. The implications for health finance are immense: by 1991 the cost of caring for AIDS patients in the United States alone is likely to be $66.4 billion. Already half California's health budget is swallowed up by AIDS related projects.

AIDS is likely to become one of the world's most pressing problems. By 1993 the World Health Organization expects to see 75,000,000 cases of full-blown AIDS worldwide.

Man-Made Disasters

Man-made disasters can result from a multitude of causes. With hindsight, it may be simple to pinpoint the fault and lay the blame, but at the time the dangers can easily be obscured. Thalidomide was hailed as a wonder drug before it was realized that it could harm the foetus when administered to women during the early stages of pregnancy. The Challenger space shuttle exploded because of a fault in one of the twin solid-fuel booster rockets. The deadly chemical cloud that floated over Bhopal resulted from a leak in a steel container in a pesticide factory.

Much can be learned from man-made disasters – better testing of drugs, siting of factories or design of football grounds – but the lessons are sometimes overlooked. Many believe that we are moving towards the greatest disaster of all, that a massive Chernobyl-style accident could blight a continent, with terrifying consequences for the rest of the world.

The Wall Street Crash 1929

The late 1920s was a boom time for the American stock market; most Americans looked forward to times of ever-increasing prosperity and saw no reason why the price of stocks and shares should not continue to climb indefinitely, so the get-rich-quick fever spread. Stocks were no longer only for the businessman and financier, for plenty of city-dwellers saw the chance of making their fortunes by investing their modest savings in the market and sitting back to wait. By 1929 there were warning signs of the trouble to come, but speculators were too busy watching the ticker tapes to notice them.

Exactly what sparked the sudden crisis in confidence and precipitated the crash has never been identified. It may be simply that, as they saw the construction industry cutting back and industrial output falling off, more and more people entertained doubts about the way the economy was going and began to sell off their investments, then others saw what was happening and rushed to follow them. The whole problem with a speculative bubble is that it takes very little to burst it. On Black Thursday, 24 October, there was a rush to sell and then, as prices began to fall, panic set in and investors scrambled to sell at any price they could get. Nearly 13,000,000 shares changed hands in one day and the floor of the Stock Exchange was a scene of frenzy, with the yelling of frantic brokers trying to sell their stocks loud enough to be heard in the street. The panic died down when news came that leading bankers had formed a pool to stabilize the market.

Prices began to climb again but, already, thousands of investors were ruined.

For a few days optimism rose, only to be dashed as the next week began. On Tuesday 16,000,000 shares changed hands, on Wednesday 11,000,000 more. For many share issues there were no buyers. Leading figures from President Hoover to John D. Rockefeller issued statements insisting that the fundamental economy of the country was sound, vainly trying to stem the tide. By the time it was decided to close the Stock Exchange for two and a half days, brokers and clerical staff had been working night and day for nearly a week and were in the last stages of nervous exhaustion.

In the last week of October, shares fell in value by 37 per cent. Stories of a great rash of suicides, with newly-impoverished speculators queuing to jump from ledges, made headlines in the British press. Though they were greatly exaggerated, there were a number of highly publicized deaths. J. J. Riordan, president of the County Trust Company, took a pistol from the teller's cage in his bank and shot himself. The head of another major company gassed himself. A ruined merchant threw himself into the river; another speculator doused himself in petrol and set himself alight. Two men who held a joint account jumped hand in hand from a high window of the Ritz Hotel and, according to music hall comedians, desk clerks in city hotels asked guests who booked rooms whether they wanted high floors for jumping or low floors for sleeping. Most of those who had lost their entire fortunes lived on to face the misery of the years that followed, as the Great Depression tightened its grip.

Below: A victim of the stock market crash tries to raise money. Right: On the day of the crash, anxious investors gather in Wall Street for the latest news.

The Great Depression 1930s

The effect of the 1929 crash on the basically unsound economy of the United States was catastrophic, but politicians and public alike were slow to realize that an era had ended and that years of deprivation lay ahead. In the following spring, President Hoover was saying confidently that the country had 'now passed the worst and with continued unity of effort we shall rapidly recover'. Other politicians were making bracing statements to the effect that less high living and more hard work would be good for everyone and that the competent now had the chance to take over from the incompetent. This belief that things would sort themselves out for the best meant that none of the decisive action necessary to stop the slump was taken.

Early in 1930 there were 3,000,000 unemployed in the United States; by 1932 the number was 11,000,000 and by the following year 13,000,000, with one in four family breadwinners out of work. In every major city, several thousand stood in line for hours each day, waiting for a meal of bread and soup to ward off starvation. It was quite normal to see men in well-cut suits left over from their wealthy days, begging for dimes on the streets. Squalid shanty towns made from wood, tarpaper and galvanized iron grew up around the edge of towns, and the inhabitants, those who could no longer afford a proper home, scavenged for food on the garbage tips. These grim, hopeless towns were called 'Hoovervilles', after a President who had set his face against federal relief programmes.

The price farmers could get for their produce dropped so steeply that many burned corn on their kitchen fires and dumped milk into ditches rather than accept it. In some areas strikes were organized and angry farmers took to the streets with pitchforks in an attempt to force the government to guarantee minimum prices. Between 1930 and 1934, around 1,000,000 farms were repossessed and angry mobs gathered to prevent foreclosures. Thousands became landless labourers, roaming the country looking for work, forced to take any meagre wages offered.

Europe, still struggling to recover from the effects of the 1914-18 war, felt the cold wind of the American recession keenly. US foreign loans were withdrawn and orders in the manufacturing sector cancelled. Britain, accustomed to depending on exports for a substantial proportion of her income, was hard hit. In 1929 there were already 1,000,000 unemployed in Britain, which had not seen the same upsurge of prosperity as the United States in the 1920s. By 1931, around 3,000,000 people were out of work. In the summer the crisis intensified as the European banks collapsed and a run on sterling followed. As an emergency measure the National Government, a coalition, was established. Britain was taken off the gold standard, the pound was devalued and protectionist measures were instituted.

All these were measures that helped to steady the economy in the long term but they had little impact for the vast army of unemployed. The government refused to heed those who maintained that the way forward was a large-scale programme of public works, so that men with jobs would have money to spend and their extra purchasing power would give the economy the boost it needed. Ministers were horrified at the idea of the extra borrowing

Left: Shanty towns, known as Hoovervilles, grew up wherever the unemployed hoped to find work. Below: Hungry New Yorkers stand in line for a free meal.

WOMEN'S
CONTINGENT
NATIONAL
HUNGER MARCH

that this scheme would entail and obsessed with the need to balance their books.

Dole money was cut and the government instituted the Means Test, aimed at reducing local authority spending. Payments were related to need and a particular family's need was assessed by an inspector. The application of the Means Test led to bitterness and resentment when those with army disability pensions found themselves denied benefit; a man who had a blind sister or elderly father living with him found that he was expected to live off his relative's pension and the few pennies a child could earn running errands for a local trader was deducted from the family's benefit. Many families went hungry and medical officers in a number of areas reported that malnutrition was resulting in abnormally high infant mortality rates and epidemics such as scarlet fever spreading like wildfire among those with little resistance. In October 1931, 2,500 people from all over the country arrived in London after marching for weeks and collecting 1,000,000 signatures on their petition asking for restitution of the dole and abolition of the Means Test. Thousands of special constables were drafted in to restrain the crowds and many people were injured as mounted police charged marchers who defended themselves with torn-up railings. Protests had little effect and between November 1931 and January 1932, more than 270,000 people had been cut off from benefit.

Meanwhile, in America's presidential campaign of 1932, Franklin D. Roosevelt told the voters: 'I pledge you, I pledge myself, to a new deal for the American people' and he promised that if he was elected, no American would starve. 'The only thing we have to fear is fear itself,' he announced. Though he took over at a desperate time, when four-fifths of the nation's banks were closed and the whole economy was on the verge of seizing up, he acted swiftly and in the 'hundred days' from March to July, 1933, he passed thirteen important measures to put the country back on its feet. Among the new schemes were provisions for re-financing farm and home mortgages, compensation for farmers who voluntarily cut production, with the aim of restoring prices to worthwhile levels, a large-scale public works programme to provide jobs, government control over the banks and a vast programme of unemployment relief. Though some of his measures were more successful than others, their sweeping and decisive nature brought a new confidence in the government and the economy and took the hopelessness out of the eyes of the unemployed.

However, events in Germany were to prove more significant in reducing unemployment than any measures taken in the United States or Britain. Germany had been devastated by the slump, with Berlin's main bank failing in 1931 and 6,000,000 out of work by the end of the year. Widespread misery and dissatisfaction with the government paved the way for the rise of Hitler, and it was World War II, with its massive need for armaments, that brought back full employment.

Above left: the women's contingent of hunger marchers leaves Holloway, in north London, on the way to Hyde Park. Left, inset: The German army set up field kitchens to help feed the unemployed.

The Tragedy of the Thalidomide Babies

In October 1957 a new 'miracle' drug developed by the German pharmaceutical firm, Chemie Grünenthal, went on sale. It was hailed as a breakthrough, a completely non-toxic tranquillizer, with no harmful side effects, that could be used safely even by infants. It was a fantastic success, marketed in over 40 countries under many different brand names. The new drug was thalidomide.

It was not until 1961 that the tragic cases of deformed babies born to mothers who had used thalidomide in the early stages of pregnancy filled the headlines. A Hamburg University professor had begun to investigate cases of babies born without limbs but with hands attached to their shoulders or feet to their hips. When he discovered that 50 such babies had been born in 15 months he found suspicious links between the births and the use of the new drug. Within weeks, thalidomide had been taken off the market.

For many families, it was already too late. Doctors normally reluctant to prescribe tranquillizers or sleeping pills to pregnant women had been lulled into a false sense of security by the safety claims made on behalf of the new drug and had often given it to women in the first three months of pregnancy to cure morning sickness. This is the time when the foetus is exceptionally vulnerable and the resulting damage was heart-breaking. Some of the babies were born without legs or arms, some had hands or feet starting from their trunks. There were eye and ear deformities, abnormalities of genitals or kidneys and, in some cases, brain damage. Some 8,000 children worldwide still live with the effects of thalidomide; there were an unknown number of stillbirths and many affected children, with serious defects of the heart, kidneys or intestines, died soon after birth.

If thalidomide had been marketed in the United States, as originally planned, with an enormous publicity campaign, there would have been thousands more victims. This extra tragedy was prevented by the strict laws on control of drugs, which say that they must be approved by the Food and Drug Administration before going on sale. In the case of thalidomide, FDA medical officer Dr Frances Kelsey was unhappy about the details supplied by the company, and continued to ask questions, including questions about possible foetal damage. When the full story was known, *The Washington Post* printed a story headed: 'Heroine of FDA keeps bad drug off market.' Only a handful of families in the United States had to suffer the trauma of producing a thalidomide baby; the mothers had been part of a clinical trial by the American company planning to produce the drug under licence.

Over 400 British thalidomide children survived. When the government refused to set up a public enquiry, parents banded together to sue the Distillers' Company (Biochemicals) Ltd, who were responsible for marketing the drug in Britain. It took years of legal wrangling, a campaign by *The Sunday Times* and intervention by consumer champion Ralph Nader, who threatened a boycott by the United

States of Distillers' company products, to win a satisfactory settlement in 1973. Since then Britain, together with several other countries, has instituted extra safeguards on the issue of new drugs and it is unlikely that doctors will ever again accept claims that any new drug is 'completely harmless.'

Above: Thalidomide victims have always been determined to show the world that, in spite of their handicap, they can do whatever they set their minds to, even if it is riding as a jockey. Left: Most children use their hands to play with toys but a thalidomide baby has to use her feet instead.

Chemical Death Clouds

Suffering in Seveso 1976

At the centre of the little Italian town of Seveso, a high fence guards piles of rubble where once stood several hundred houses of prosperous local families. It is deserted now and the area has to stay sealed for ever, a constant reminder of the accident at the Icmesa chemical plant owned by Hoffman La Roche of Switzerland in 1976. The suffering people of Seveso, of course, need no reminder: many of them will bear the physical and psychological scars for life.

On a hot July day, an explosion at the plant, which made agricultural herbicides, produced a freak chemical reaction releasing a deadly cloud of tetrachlorodibenzodioxin which hung menacingly over houses and farmlands. Within the next 24 hours, plants and trees in the affected area withered, animals died and children developed painful skin rashes.

The local people had no idea that the chemicals used in the factory were potentially dangerous and at first no one understood what was happening. It was 10 days before the regional government declared that the area had been polluted by dioxin; then soldiers cordoned off the factory and the sale or consumption of locally produced meat, vegetables, fruit and milk was forbidden. Many people lost all their possessions when the centre of the town was sealed off permanently and the houses demolished.

Dioxin is an active ingredient in the defoliant which, used by the American forces, laid waste great areas of Vietnam. In tiny amounts it kills animals but no one knows for certain what the long-term effects on humans might be and there are fears that it might cause cancers and other disorders in those who were exposed to the Seveso cloud. The full effects may never be known because 11,000 fled the town once they knew what had happened. Some came back to be rehoused in 'safe' areas but many never returned and attempts to trace them through doctors all over the country failed. However, the immediate effects were only too obvious. Over 400 children developed chloracne, a recurring eruption of painful, weeping boils all over the body and many were left disfigured for life. Five decontamination workers contracted liver disease, in spite of their protective clothing and brief shifts. Several hundred women sought and obtained permission for abortions, normally against the law in a strictly Roman Catholic country, and the birth rate among those who remained in Seveso dropped dramatically. Few were willing to take the risk that their babies might be born with deformities.

Officials admitted that their major problem was knowing so little about what they were dealing with. They could only guess at how far the chemical effects had spread; there was consternation when traces of dioxin were found in the mud of a street in Milan, 21 km (13 miles) away. There was strenuous disagreement over what should be done to decontaminate the area. The regional health

COMUNI MEDA E SEVESO

ZONA INFESTATA

da

sostanze tossiche

DIVIETO

TOCCARE O INGERIRE PRODOTTI ORTOFRUTTICOLI, EVITANDO CONTATTI CON VEGETAZIONE, TERRA E ERBE IN GENERE.

L'UFFICIALE SANITARIO   I SINDACI

Above: The city of Seveso died after the deadly cloud of dioxin blanketed its streets; no-one can now live in the worst affected area. Left: A group of workers leave for the contamination zone, clad from head to foot in protective clothing.

officer, Professor Ghetti, said: 'We should have burnt down the entire poisoned zone. What has happened here is on the same scale as Hiroshima. It is one of the most gruesome catastrophes in the world'. Other experts, however, argued that these tactics would be far too risky as the dioxin would be carried into the air by the smoke and would pollute other areas.

Death in Bhopal 1984

In the early hours of the morning on 2 December 1984 a yellowish-white cloud of gas, leaking from a storage tank at the Union Carbide (India) factory in the city of Bhopal, spread out across the neighbouring shanty town, on into the old quarter of the city. It carried death with it: many died where they slept, others woke choking and vomiting, their throats and eyes burning, and staggered helplessly into the street to die.

Within 40 minutes the cloud of methyl isocyanate, a chemical used in the manufacture of insecticides, had spread over 40 km (25 miles) of the city. Worst affected were the hundreds of families in the makeshift homes of wood and tarpaulin, with corrugated iron roofs, which had grown up around the factory walls and which offered no protection from the choking fumes. As the thick mist settled over the nearby railway station, passengers and staff alike rolled on the ground, frothing at the mouth and vomiting. The station superintendent signalled an approaching train to drive on without stopping, saving the lives of hundreds of passengers before being overcome by the gas himself.

Most of those who could still walk, or stagger, piled out into the streets, trying to flee the lethal cloud, and roads already littered with dead animals became a seething mass of terrified humanity. Within the first hour the hospital was full to overflowing with the injured, lying on tables, benches and the floor. Doctors set up makeshift clinics outside and treated the crowds of victims as best they could. By 07.00, 20,000 patients had arrived at the hospital and the dead were laid out in rows on the lawns, their faces covered with white cloths. Three thousand people died as a result of the accident and 40,000 were seriously injured. Many were left with damaged lungs, sight problems and bronchial ailments; the rate of miscarriages trebled, the infant mortality rate doubled among babies born to mothers who has been exposed to the gas. Many were left with long-term psychological complaints.

The leak was caused when a tank valve malfunctioned after an increase in pressure. Union Carbide, one of the world's largest corporations, was later to suggest sabotage but the report of government scientists blamed the accident on faulty design, poor construction and a 'lack of appreciation of potential hazards'. When Warren Anderson, president and chief executive of Union Carbide since 1977, flew to Bhopal on 6 December, he was arrested, along with the Indian executives of the plant, and charged with criminal negligence and conspiracy, but he was released a few hours later. At a press conference when he returned to the United States, he said 'The name of the game is not to nail me to the wall but to provide for the people'. A long, legal wrangle between the Indian government and Union Carbide was to follow, providing little comfort for the survivors of the world's worst-ever industrial accident.

When the plant was reopened a few days after the disaster in order to neutralize the chemicals in the remaining tanks and make it safe in the long term, there was a mass exodus from Bhopal as up to 200,000 fled the old city, leaving it like a ghost town until after the process was completed.

Right: The local people who lived alongside the Union Carbide plant in Bhopal did not realize the danger until the morning of the chemical leak. Below: The accident was to kill and injure many thousands and widespread rescue work was necessary.

The Jonestown Suicides 1978

One of the strangest of the world's disasters happened in a remote commune in Guyana, South America, when over 900 members of a fanatical Californian cult took part in a mass suicide ritual, swallowing a lethal mix of cyanide and a soft drink. The mixture was ladled from a large tub by the commune's doctor and nurse; members lined up to collect their poisoned drink, singing gospel songs. Parents spooned it into the mouths of babies, adults drank and wrapped their arms around one another to stay close in death. When Guyanese soldiers arrived the next day they found the body of the cult's leader, James Warren Jones, lying across the altar, a bullet through his head. Some bodies lay at the edge of the clearing, near the trees, with bullets in their backs; they had not been allowed to decide against suicide but had been mown down as they tried to flee.

Forty-six-year-old Jones, who had a degree in education from the University of Indiana, had attracted followers by preaching a gospel of racial integration that would create a classless society. He had prospered in San Francisco, winning support from a number of prominent politicans and often preaching to a congregation of 5,000. Then came allegations that he was using his power over cult members to swell the funds of the ministry, that he faked 'faith cures' and presided over bizarre sex rituals. Some defec-

tors spoke out, saying that they had pretended to be blind or crippled, only enabled to see or walk again when Jones laid hands on them. Others claimed that they had been pressured into signing all their money over to him. At one point the ministry's holdings were said to stand at $5 million. Eventually Jones moved his commune to Guyana, setting up a community called Jonestown on a tract of savannah grassland, surrounded by jungle and heavy bush, where they would be far removed from criticism and interference.

Then, in November 1978, a party led by Californian Congressman Leo Ryan and including press reporters and photographers arrived in Guyana to investigate reports

Right: When the authorities arrived in Jonestown, they found the ground littered with bodies of men, women and children. Below: Jim Jones, the charismatic leader of a fanatical cult that led to death.

that young people were being held against their will, beaten and abused when they did not obey Jones's orders to the letter. Ryan had pressured the US State Department to persuade the Guyanese government to let him fly to Jonestown to talk to the cult members himself. He guaranteed protection for all those who wanted to leave and 20 commune members asked to go with him. The party was preparing to leave from Port Kaituma airport, 13 km (8 miles) from Jonestown, when they were ambushed. A tractor drove out of the undergrowth onto the concrete and gunmen opened fire from it, moving in to shoot victims already lying on the ground at point-blank range. Among the dead were Congressman Ryan, NBC reporter

Don Harris and cameraman Robert Brown, who had continued filming after the carnage began, only stopping when hit by a bullet.

An eyewitness claimed that Jones ordered the mass suicide when he heard that some of Ryan's party had escaped, and realized that the authorities would soon be arriving. Jones had planned the final ritual long before and told his followers what they must do if the existence of the commune was ever threatened. Many changed into their best Sunday clothes before gathering in front of the altar to hear Jones talking about the dignity and beauty of death and telling them: 'We were too good for this world. Now come with me and I will take you to a better place.'

Trouble in Space 1967, 1971, 1986

Before 1967, the space capsule was the safest form of transport available to man. The amount of money and expertise poured into America's space research had ensured that the programme was statistically safer than driving on a freeway in the rush hour. The world had watched spellbound as American astronauts and Soviet cosmonauts circled the earth in giant rockets, walked in space and returned safely to earth.

Then, on 27 January, the US space programme claimed its first victims. The three man crew of the Apollo One spacecraft, members of the Apollo project to send the first men safely to the moon, reported for duty at the Kennedy Space Centre, Florida. Gus Grissom, Ed White and Roger Chaffee were to spend the day strapped into the cockpit of the command module, repeating over and over again the lift-off drill they would be using in a few weeks' time. Five hours of routine drill followed before a ground control technician noticed a malfunction, then immediately afterwards came Ed White's voice saying: 'Fire in the cockpit'. The horrified controllers heard seven seconds of 'clawing and pounding' on the hatch, the Roger Chaffee was pleading 'We're on fire . . . get us out of here.'

Minutes later the hatch was opened, but all three astro-nauts were dead. A spark, probably caused by a loose wire, had ignited in the oxygen-rich atmosphere of the cabin. NASA had favoured the pure oxygen atmosphere over the safer oxygen and nitrogen mixture chosen by the Russians because it meant they could do without weighty and cumbersome equipment, though some scientists had issued grim warnings about the fire hazards. In Apollo One, the tiny spark had turned the cabin into an inferno in which the astronauts had no chance of survival.

Disaster was to strike the Soviet space programme four years later, as a shock ending to a highly successful mission. On 19 April 1971 the permanent space station Salyut One had been launched into orbit, followed by the docking of the Soyuz Eleven capsule with three cosmonauts on board. Twenty-four days later Soyuz was disengaged from the space station and it began its carefully controlled journey back to earth. Though radio contact was lost on re-entry, no one was unduly worried and after Soyuz had made a perfect touchdown, the recovery crew opened the hatch ready to greet the triumphant cosmonauts. Inside, the three men were dead. They had suffocated after an air valve in the main hatch jarred open and, their muscles weakened by prolonged weightlessness, they had not sufficient strength to close it again.

In the meantime, in spite of the setbacks, the space programme had forged ahead and men had walked on the moon. Now NASA was looking ahead to a space station from which a manned mission to Mars could be launched.

Below: Astronauts prepare for the first manned Apollo mission. Right above: The Apollo One spacecraft after the fire. Right below: The funeral of Vladimir Komarov, killed in the Soyuz capsule.

TV CAMERA
ATTACH

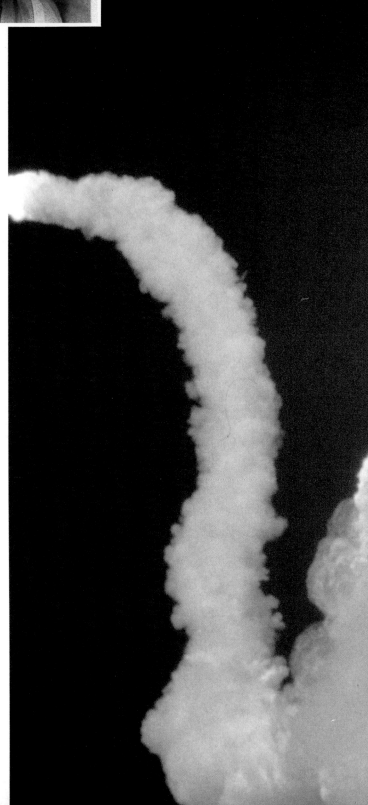

**Right: The space shuttle explodes soon after the launch.
Above: The shocked faces of the onlookers.**

One of the first steps was the development of the space shuttle, a re-usable commuter 'truck' to carry equipment into orbit, launch satellites and carry out routine work in space.

The *Challenger* 51L mission of January 1986 should have been straightforward and trouble-free. Its objective was to launch a tracking and relay satellite and also to observe Halley's comet as it reached the nearest point to the sun – a chance that would not come again for 76 years. Commanding *Challenger* crew was Francis Scobee, Vietnam veteran and test pilot. His six member crew were Navy commander Michael Smith, Air Force major Ellison Onizuka, laser development specialist Ronald McNair, electrical engineer Judith Resnek, who had become the second American woman in space in 1984, engineer Greg Jarvis and teacher Christa McAuliffe. Mrs McAuliffe, the first private citizen chosen to go into space, had been selected from 11,000 would-be astronauts in NASA's 'Teacher in Space' project. Her enthusiastic, extrovert personality meant that she would be able to communicate the knowledge she gained to a young audience; she said she intended to 'humanize the technology of the space age.'

Her lawyer husband, her parents and two children, as well as a contingent of her pupils, were among the crowds who assembled to watch the launch on Tuesday 28 January. The mission had already been postponed three times and that morning, there were still doubts about its advisability. The temperature overnight had been well below freezing and icicles hung round the launch pad. No previous shuttle had been launched in such low temperatures but eventually the takeoff was scheduled for 11.38.

Spectators watched enthralled as *Challenger* rose on its column of fire into a brilliant blue sky. When the shuttle exploded into a huge fireball at a height of 13 km (8 miles), no one could believe what they were seeing. Clouds of smoke and flame made strange patterns in the sky. The crowd fell silent as a voice over the loudspeaker said: 'Obviously a major malfunction.' It was the first time American astronauts had been lost during a mission and the worst accident in 25 years of manned spaceflight.

Above: The crew of the shuttle *Challenger* could have no idea of the tragedy that would follow lift-off.

As NASA teams embarked on the grim task of retrieving the debris from the Atlantic, President Reagan appointed a commission under former Secretary of State William Rogers to investigate, and the resulting 256 page report was a damning indictment of NASA management. Vital engineering considerations had been overlooked in the race to maintain an ambitious programme of launches each year.

Some engineers had given advance warnings that the joints between the segments of the booster casings, sealed with two rubber O-rings, might fail under certain conditions and this was exactly what happened to *Challenger*. Film of the launch showed that 58 seconds into the flight, a jet of flame from the right hand booster rocket was already licking round the fuel tank. What had happened was that the O-rings had become brittle in the low temperatures and no longer sealed the joint properly. As the speed built up and strong cross-winds buffeted the shuttle, the joints fractured with devastating results. The conclusion was that the shuttle should never have been launched at all under such conditions.

A major shakeup in the management of NASA followed, as well as modifications in the design of the shuttle and hopefully the lesson learned is that specialist engineers should have the final say in whether a launch should proceed or not. As President Reagan said in a television broadcast on the night of the tragedy: 'There will be more shuttle flights . . . more teachers in space. Nothing ends here. Our hope and our journeys continue.'

Football Tragedies 1964, 1971, 1985

A 45,000 strong crowd packed the stadium in Lima, Peru, for the vital 1964 soccer match between Argentina and Peru. Feelings ran high as the Peruvians watched Argentina score a goal, while their own team were apparently unable to steer the match their way. Then, with only two minutes to go, Peru equalized. The ecstatic cheers turned to yells of fury when the referee announced a foul and disallowed the goal. Two spectators ran onto the pitch, intent on attacking the referee, and several dozen policemen raced after them. The game was abandoned as more and more incensed spectators invaded the pitch and mounted police moved in to try to clear the stadium, herding the fans towards the exits and, as the mood turned more and more ugly, using tear gas and dogs in their attempt to control the crowds.

The stands were a mass of struggling bodies: some fighting the police, some setting fire to benches, most scrambling in panic for the exits. As the crowds reached the street they overturned cars, set light to buildings and looted stores. Behind them, in the stadium, they left a trail of bodies, most trampled to death or suffocated. Over 300 died and at least 500 more were injured, and the Peruvian government declared a state of emergency.

Similar scenes have become depressingly familiar to those concerned with British football matches. The Ibrox Park tragedy on 2 January 1971, which killed 66 people and injured 100, happened, like that in Peru, at the end of the game. Thousands of fans at the Rangers v. Celtic match were on their way out, believing that Celtic had won, when Rangers scored an unexpected equalizing goal. As the great cheer went up, many of those who were leaving tried to fight their way back, only to meet a solid wall of people on their way out. In the crush that followed, the railings of the stairway gave way; people began falling, others fell on top of them. A policeman, hearing screams and running to the scene, found: 'a pile of bodies about 10 feet high all laid the say way with their faces towards me – a wall of faces, some with their tongues lolling out. . . The injuries of some of those who had been crushed right under the barrier were horrible to see. We came away with our boots, socks and the bottom of our trousers soaked in blood.'

Two major football stadium disasters followed closely in 1985. In May, 56 people were killed when a sudden fire engulfed a wooden stand at Bradford City's ground, in northern England. The match was nearing half-time when the first few tongues of flame were seen, after a dropped cigarette ignited rubbish accumulated behind the seats. Within two minutes the fire had spread the entire length of the stand, swiftly consuming the plastic seats and spreading to the wood and felt roof. When fans tried to flee they

Left: The steep steps of Ibrox Park stadium after the disaster, when supporters were crushed against the steel barriers. Below: At Bradford City, fire engulfed a stand within a couple of minutes.

found exits locked and later charred bodies were found jammed up against locked turnstiles. Those who could climb the high barrier wall escaped onto the pitch and parents started throwing children over to safety. Policemen dashed repeatedly into the stand, rescuing those whose clothes were already on fire, rolling them over on the grass to extinguish the flames. The fire led to an official enquiry into the safety precautions and standards at all English clubs.

Less than three weeks later, crowd violence erupted at Belgium's Heysel Stadium before the European Cup Final between Liverpool and Juventus of Turin had even started. Trouble began when the English Liverpool fans broke the inadequate barriers separating them from rival Juventus supporters. Most of the 41 people who were killed were crushed when a wall collapsed under the weight of Juventus supporters trying to escape. The stampede continued even after it was obvious that people had been hurt and killed. Appeals for calm were broadcast to the 58,000 crowd in English, Italian, French and Dutch, while Red Cross and emergency hospital services tried to help the injured. Over 400 people were hurt, many with multiple fractures or damage to lungs, liver and spleen.

The Heysel tragedy made football hooliganism into an international issue. It resulted in an indefinite ban on English clubs taking part in European competitions as well as tighter controls on alcohol, closed circuit television was instituted for surveillance at matches and pressure began for computerized membership schemes.

Violence was not to blame for the accident at the Hillsborough ground in Sheffield when 95 people died, teenage girls and children among them, and more than 200 were injured. The FA Cup semi-final was being played between Liverpool and Nottingham Forest and rival fans had been carefully separated at different ends of the ground. The allocation of space was a sore point from the beginning: though the Liverpool club had twice as many members as Nottingham, they had been allocated the less spacious end of the ground. When between 3,000 and 4,000 Liverpool fans arrived only 10 minutes before the match was due to start, the crush at that end of the ground was so great that a police horse was lifted from its feet. A senior policeman, seeing that the situation was becoming dangerous, ordered that a gate which was normally opened only at the end of the match should be unlocked.

As the teams came out and a great roar went up, the fans outside surged forward uncontrollably, so that those already inside were knocked to the ground and trampled on or forced up against the metal perimeter fence, erected to prevent hooligans from invading the pitch. Most of the fatalities were the result of asphyxiation; those crushed against the barriers like caged animals were unable to breathe and quickly lost consciousness. Some of those caught in the crowd later reported seeing an old man in the throes of a heart attack and a young girl suffocated as her face was rammed into the shoulders of the person in front, but they were unable to move their arms to save them.

'There was a great surge from behind and we were just carried along until we hit the fences!' said one fan. 'All round us people were screaming. There were people lying on the ground being kicked and trampled – they were just dying there at our feet and there was nothing we could do to help them.'

Below: Soccer fans struggle to get free after the collapse of a wall in Heysel stadium. Above right: The horror of Hillsborough. Below right: Fans filled the Hillsborough stadium with flowers and momentoes.

Nuclear Accidents 1957, 1979, 1986

ince the birth of the nuclear industry in the 1940s there have been warnings of the horrific dangers of accidents from its opponents. What happened in Chernobyl in the USSR in April 1986, when a terrible fire released some seven tonnes of highly radioactive material into the atmosphere, seemed to confirm all their worst fears.

The world had come near to nuclear catastrophe before. At Britain's Windscale plant fire engulfed a plutonium production reactor on 8 October 1957 and blazed out of control until the morning of 11 October, coming close to causing a full-scale disaster before it was extinguished. There was no evacuation of houses near the plant and the British public was told nothing until the alarm was over. Later reports indicated that more than 250 people were likely to have contracted thyroid cancer as a result of radioactive discharges at the time.

Left: The UK reprocessing plant at Windscale (now renamed Sellafield) was the scene of an accident in 1957. Below: Engineers enter the containment building after the incident at Three Mile Island.

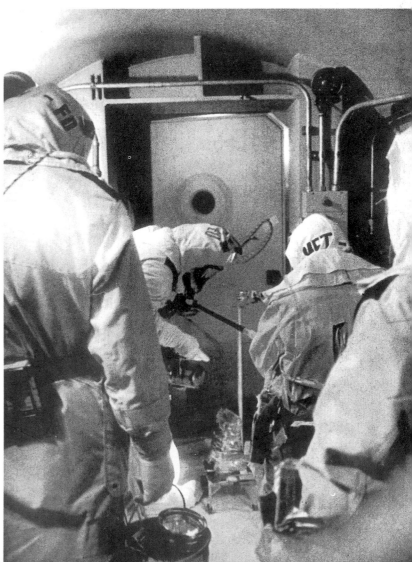

In 1982 an American government report showed that 169 incidents which could have led to a major catastrophe had occurred in the USA in the decade from 1969 alone but the country's closest shave was to come on 28 March 1979 at Three Mile Island, near Harrisburg, Pa., when the uranium core of one of the plant's pressurized water reactors overheated and radiation inside the reactor building reached levels 75 times above those required to kill a human being. There was much subsequent criticism of the handling of the incident by the authorities, who were slow to give information and begin evacuation.

The results of the world's worst nuclear accident were first detected in Sweden, then in Finland, Denmark and Norway, where alarming increases in radioactivity were monitored. Swedish experts deduced that the leak had come from Chernobyl and their suspicions were confirmed by US spy satellites.

It was to be 18 days before Soviet leader Gorbachev informed the nation about the accident and its effects on television, admitting that 299 people were being treated in hospital. Later reports have shown that, though the immediate area was evacuated soon after the accident, the citizens of Kiev, 100 km (62 miles) south of Chernobyl, were given no warnings until after patients suffering from severe burns and radiation sickness began arriving at the hospital and rumours were causing panic. As the Soviet authorities realized the extent of the contamination, a quarter of a million schoolchildren were evacuated from Kiev to safer areas.

Meltdown was avoided by encasing the damaged re-actor in concrete but by then virtually every country in Europe, both east and west, was contaminated by radioactivity. One of the worst 'hot spots' was in north east Poland, where radioactivity was 500 times the normal level. In parts of East Germany they were 100 times normal. Many countries imposed restrictions on the movement of fresh food and grazing animals such as cows and sheep, which might have been contaminated.

Experts differ in their estimates of the number of additional cancers that might be caused by the Chernobyl incident. The most conservative estimate is 10,000 cancers in the Soviet Union and 1,000 in the rest of Europe, with about half that number resulting in deaths. Other experts suggest that the total might be ten times higher than that. Since even small levels of exposure to radiation can weaken the immune system, contamination is likely to damage the health of several million people.

The accident at Chernobyl caused a crisis of confidence in the world's nuclear industry and led to large-scale anti-nuclear demonstrations in many European countries. The official enquiry found that human error was the chief cause of the accident but also pointed out basic faults in the design of the reactor. Changes have been made as a result of Chernobyl, but many more people than ever before are now convinced that there is no such thing as a safe nuclear reactor.

Left and below: After the tragedy at Chernobyl, the damaged reactor was encased in concrete but it was too late to prevent the spread of contamination.

Bursting Dams 1889, 1963

Those living close to major dams are only too aware of the possibility of a fault and the tragedy that could follow any breach in the dam walls. There had been concern over the state of the South Fork Dam near Johnstown in Pennsylvania for years before its final failure. It was a massive structure, 280 m (930 ft) long, 82 m (270 ft) wide and 21 m (72 ft) high with a 3 km (2 mile) long reservoir behind it. It had been built by the State in 1852 as part of a canal and rail transport system, since made redundant by the advance of the railroad across the mountains. The dam was sold off and the lake stocked with fish for visiting sportsmen but when repairs were needed, the owners settled for a cheap patch-up job. To add to the danger, the top of the dam was levelled so that a road could be built across the lake.

When weeks of rain in May 1889 culminated in a fierce downpour, with 40 cm (16 in) of rain falling within 24 hours, the dam was in no state to withstand the onslaught and the water tore a hole in its side and cascaded down towards the town below, gathering debris of uprooted trees and smashed houses, tossing heavy locomotives high in the air as though they were toys. The water rampaged through Johnstown unchecked until it reached the great stone railway bridge in the centre of town. The bridge held but debris piled up behind it, forming a 21 m (70 ft) high tower in which trapped men, women and children struggled helplessly. The contents of a freight car caught fire and the flames licked hungrily at the pile of smashed wood. Within minutes it became an inferno, roasting its victims alive and blazing for three days. The lethal combination of water and fire killed 2,200 people, wiping out 100 families completely.

Poor maintenance is one obvious reason for the collapse of a dam but there are many others. Some of the most spectacular failures have been caused by water undermining the foundations – the reason given for the destruction of the St Francis Dam in California in 1928. Others failed because they were sited over geological faults, like the Teton Dam in Idaho, which was breached even before its offical opening.

The exhaustive enquiry following the bursting of the Vaiont Dam in Italy decided that the site was badly chosen. Engineers and geologists working on the dam, constructed to provide hydro-electric power, had been aware of movements and rockfalls on Mount Toc, towering 180 m (6,000 ft) above the reservoir but had underestimated the danger. On the night of 9 October 1963, following heavy rains, a vast avalanche swept down the slopes of Mount Toc and thousands of tons of rock and earth crashed into the lake, so that a huge wave of water rose over the top of the dam and poured into the valley below, engulfing the villages in its path and killing 1,190 people.

Those living below the dam were given no warning and only those whose homes were on high ground at the edge of the valley had any chance of survival. By morning all that could be seen was a vast, silent desert of mud and rock, with the remains of a building rising up here and there. It took time for those outside to hear the full facts: all telephone and telegraph lines were down, the railroads were destroyed and the roads turned into swamps. When the Italian Minister of Public Works was finally able to reach the area he described it as a 'truly biblical disaster . . . like Pompeii before the excavations began'. Five days later the search for bodies was still going on, but many were buried nameless; all their relatives were gone and there was no one left to identify them.

Below: Rescue workers search for bodies after the waters of the Vaiont dam engulfed the valley below. Right: Italian soldiers remove the dead, working quickly because of fears of a disease epidemic.

Oil Spills

Torrey Canyon and Amoco Cadiz 1967 and 1978

Britain faced the most serious oil pollution threat this century when the giant oil tanker the *Torrey Canyon* ran aground on a reef between the Scilly Isles and Land's End on 18 March 1967. The 297 m (975 ft) tanker, owned by a US company incorporated in Liberia, was on charter to BP and bound for Milford Haven with a cargo of 117,000 tons of Kuwaiti oil. Rocks tore the bottom out of the ship and oil began to stream out. Over the next six days, some 30,000 tons of oil flowed into the sea, causing an oil slick covering 675 square kilometres (260 square

miles). All attempts to save the *Torrey Canyon* failed, and two days later she broke her back and tens of thousands more tons of oil escaped into the sea. An emergency operation was mounted on 28 and 29 March, with Royal Air Force bombers dropping vast amounts of explosives, as well as aviation fuel and napalm, to sink the wreck and burn off any remaining fuel.

The splendid beaches and coves of Cornwall were polluted for a distance of 233 km (145 miles) and 2,000 servicemen, joined by as many volunteers, worked to spray detergent on the beaches and sea, with US Air Force troops from British bases joining the fight. Beaches on the Brittany coast and the Channel Islands were also hit, but by the summer holiday season the sands were clean

Below: The *Torrey Canyon* broke up in heavy seas off Land's End, after running aground. Right: Thousands of helpers were mobilized after the *Amoco Cadiz* spilled her oil off the coast of Brittany.

again. In the long run, the birds were the worst sufferers, with wildlife experts estimating that 25,000 had been killed in Cornwall alone.

Worse was to come in March 1978 when the *Amoco Cadiz* lost 223,000 tons of crude oil in the sea. The tanker, belonging to the US owned Amoco International Oil Co., was making her way from the Persian Gulf to Rotterdam, on what was to be her last voyage, when the ship's steering gear broke down in heavy seas. Attempts to tow the tanker failed and she drifted onto the rocks, breaking her back and disgorging oil. In the subsequent enquiry the ship's Italian captain was criticized for his 'inexcusable delay' in asking for help. If he had radioed for assistance as soon as the steering gear failed, the *Amoco Cadiz* might have been towed safely to shore.

French contingency plans for dealing with spillages had been made with the idea of disposing of 30,000 tons, not with the contents of a supertanker, and the people of Brit-

tany were furious to find how ineffectual the mopping up operation was in the early stages. Oil covered 400 km (250 miles) of shoreline, settling as a sticky black mousse. It was too thick to be piped away and the government would not allow detergent to be used onshore because of possible damage to crops and oyster beds, so 'Operation Teaspoon' was mounted to dispose of the mess, as little as a teaspoon at a time. Between 5,000 and 8,000 people a day, including troops, firemen and public works employees, were deployed to scrape up the oil manually, so that it could be removed in drums and buried in special pits. Once that was done, high pressure hoses were used to spray the rocks. The vast cleanup operation and the restricted use of chemicals meant that the wildlife of the area suffered less than originally predicted, though something like 22,000 birds perished. The oyster industry was also badly hit, with millions of oysters either dead or contaminated.

Alaska Polluted 1989

America's worst oil spill happened in the lonely, spectacular state of Alaska, when the *Exxon Valdez* ran aground in Prince William Sound, 40 km (25 miles) out of the port of Valdez in March 1989. Coastguards reported that the ship's officers had radioed for permission to leave their shipping channel because of the dangers of ice. They were given clearance to steer east to another channel about 1.6 km (1 mile) away but when the tanker hit a reef it was outside any of the normal shipping lanes. At 12.27 on Good Friday the vessel's captain transmitted the message: 'Evidently we're losing some oil and we're going to be here a while.'

In all, 11,000,000 gallons of oil spilled from the crippled tanker, turning the beaches and coves into graveyards for the region's birds and animals. Within 10 days, the pollution had spread over 1,295 square kilometres (500 square miles) of sea and 1,290 km (800 miles) of coastline, with many beaches thick with oil up to 90 m (100 yards) above the tideline.

Environmentalists who had opposed the routing of the Alaskan pipeline through the Sound found their worst fears fulfilled and were bitter in their criticism of the slow and inadequate cleaning-up operation. The contingency plans filed by the Alyeska Pipeline Company, formed by the companies operating in the area, had promised a 'quick and effective' response in the event of a spillage. In fact, the barge that should have been on standby was out of service after storm damage and instead of taking five

hours to begin the clean-up operation, it took 15 to get it under way. By the time all the necessary equipment was in place the weather, calm and still for two days after the spill, had turned stormy, and winds fierce enough to tear off part of the roof from the terminal building at Valdez airport hampered cleansing efforts. A fortnight later only one fifth of the spillage had been recovered and oil had been found 112 km (70 miles) away. The president of the Exxon Shipping Company, owners of the tanker, was quoted as saying: 'The slick is moving like its on a super highway. We've got a real mess on our hands.'

Within hours of the spill, environmental officers were collecting the sticky black carcasses of seabirds who had fallen exhausted, their feathers glued together. Estimates of the numbers of birds killed ranges from 20,000 to 40,000. Thousands of sea otters died too, often frozen to death because the oil robbed their fur of its natural insulation. Deer and bears who foraged on the shore were poisoned by eating oiled birds or animals.

The full environmental cost will never be known. The herring shoals making their way to the open sea and the annual salmon run through the Sound may well be blighted. Millions of migratory seabirds pass through the Sound every year, and eating contaminated fish is a death sentence for them. When a bird dies from eating contaminated fish, it is likely to be eaten by another creature, which in turn dies and poisons any animal that feeds on it. Experts think that it could be 10 years before Prince William Sound can recover, but for the birds and animals, death by pollution will have spread far beyond the immediate area.

Right and below: The Alaskan oil spill, the worst ever experienced in the US, had tragic consequences for the bird and marine life of the area.

Tragedies of Air, Sea and Rail

Major disasters of sea, rail and air are mercifully rare, but when they do happen, the number of casualties can be such that they brand themselves into international memory. Some, like the sinking of the Titanic or the Hindenburg bursting into flames, are so well-known that they have almost turned into legends of the 20th century. Even in more recent decades, terrible incidents like the shooting down of the Korean 747 or the bomb that exploded aboard the Pan Am flight over Lockerbie have sent shock waves throughout the world.

The causes of so many transport disasters can be traced back to a moment's carelessness or to a chain of human error that leads to inevitable tragedy – a discarded cigarette aboard the Morro Castle, the bow doors left open on the Herald of Free Enterprise or a poorly maintained gas pipeline alongside railway lines in the USSR. Hopefully, lessons learned from accidents like these will, in future, lead to better standards of safety for all travellers.

Sea Disasters

The Sinking of the Titanic 1912

The *SS Titanic* set sail on her maiden voyage from Southampton, England, to New York on Wednesday, 10 April 1912 with a passenger list of 1,308 including the rich and famous of both the United States and Britain, probably worth more than $250 million between them. It was the largest, most luxurious ship ever built, with engines capable of moving the 46,000 ton vessel at a speed well over 23 knots. The thick steel hull had a double bottom and was divided into 16 watertight compartments; she was considered the ultimate in marine design, the unsinkable ship. The *Titanic* was equipped with every modern convenience, from the first-ever shipboard swimming pool to the new radio instrument, the Marconi Telegraph.

The *Titanic* headed out into the North Atlantic under a clear sky, but the temperature was dropping fast and on Sunday 14 April, the Marconi men received radio messages warning of the danger of icebergs. However, the ship steamed on at a steady 22 knots. At 22.40, the lookout spotted an iceberg dead ahead. The first officer ordered the helm to starboard and, at first, it seemed as though the ship would shave past safely. Many passengers did not even notice the grinding noise below the waterline, as the ice tore into the hull of the ship. There was no crash, no jarring; even when the engines stopped, there was curiosity rather than alarm; everyone knew the ship was unsinkable. Some of the steerage passengers even staged a 'snowball' fight with the pieces of ice littering the deck.

However, down below the iceberg had torn a gash 90 m (300 ft) long, right across the first five watertight compartments. The icy Atlantic·water was flooding in and the ship was beginning to sink. Captain Edward Smith ordered the lifeboats to be prepared and told the radio operators to start transmitting a call for help. Meanwhile the stewards went from cabin to cabin telling passengers to report on deck in their lifejackets. Though most passengers obeyed, some remained convinced that it was merely an inconvenient safety drill and stayed where they were.

Even as the boats were swung out with the order 'Women and children only', the passengers remained calm and unruffled, as though no one could believe there was any real danger. Compared to the fragile looking boats, the ship seemed so safe and permanent. But the captain knew that the ship was sinking lower all the time and that, as her bows dipped deeper, it would be more and more difficult to lower the lifeboats. he also knew that there were sufficient boats for only a little over half the passengers on board.

The ship's musicians gathered on deck and, as the boats pulled away, the strains of a hymn, 'Nearer My God to Thee' drifted across the water. Male passengers, left behind on the deck as their wives and children disappeared into the darkness, joined in the singing. Some

Below: The *Titanic*, hailed as the most luxurious ship in the world, steams proudly out of port on her ill-fated maiden voyage. Right: The ship's captain, Edward Smith, was an experienced sailor but in the enquiry following the tragedy he was criticized for complacency in his handling of the ship.

"BE BRITISH" : The Last Words of the " Titanic's " Captain.

"They that go down to the sea in ships, that do business in great waters."—Psalm cvii.

COMMANDER EDWARD J. SMITH, R.N.R.
From a portrait taken in New York. Reproduced by kind permission of Mrs. Smith

Born in the Year 1853

Nothing is here for tears, nothing to wail
Or knock the breast, no weakness, no contempt,

Dispraise or blame ; nothing but well and fair,
And what may quiet us in a death so noble. Samson Agonistes

Died April 15, 1912

passengers remained calm and detached, others panicked as the last boats were lowered. Some women refused to leave their husbands. When an officer ordered Mrs Isador Straus into a boat, she said 'We have been together all these years and I'll not leave him now.' There were skirmishes as men tried to fight their way onto the boats; three men jumped into a boat as it was being lowered, dislocating the ribs of a woman passenger. Women hid a 14-year-old boy with their skirts but an officer ordered him back aboard, telling him 'For God's sake, be a man.' Small children and babies wrapped in blankets were thrown in, to be caught by those already in the boats. A Belgian immigrant, Julius Sop, dived into the water and swam to a lifeboat, only to have an officer threaten to shoot him if he climbed aboard; another man who was trying to pull himself out of the water was hit over the head with an oar. An American woman saved him, pushing the oar aside, saying 'I can't see the poor fellow die. We might as well all go together.'

Though the Cunard liner *Carpathia* had received the distress call and signalled that she was coming to the rescue, it was obvious that she would not arrive in time. Shortly after the last lifeboat was launched, the *Titanic* began to shake as the sea flooded the first class quarters. Hundreds of immigrants clustered round a priest on their knees, praying as the water rose around them. In the gentlemen's lounge on A deck, men in evening dress continued to play cards on steeply slanting tables. In the third class lounge an English woman with a baby on her knee went on playing the piano.

Those in the lifeboats watched as the great liner, still with lights ablaze, dipped forward in the water. There was a rumbling explosion and then another; the *Titanic*'s stern lifted until it was almost vertical. Then suddenly the lights were extinguished and there was a great roar as the engines and boilers tore free and fell towards the bows. The giant liner slid quietly downwards, the waters closing over her.

The water was full of survivors screaming for help. Some were hauled into the lifeboats but most died in the icy water. On fully laden lifeboats the passengers, terrified of being swamped, rowed away as fast as they could, singing 'Pull for the shore, sailor' to drown the cries. The *Carpathia* arrived at 04.00 hours to rescue 705 people from the boats. The *Californian*, which had been only 30 km (19 miles) away from the *Titanic*, arrived shortly afterwards. She had not received the distress calls because her radio had been shut down for the night and no one aboard had seen the *Titanic*'s distress rockets; the captain learned of the tragedy from another vessel hours after the *Titanic* had sunk.

The world was stunned by the extent of the tragedy: nearly 1,500 people were lost, mostly crew and male passengers. The US Senate enquiry that followed criticized the captain for his over-confidence and indifference to danger; the lack of lifeboats, and the crew's inexperience over proper safety measures. The enquiry resulted in the formation of the International Ice Patrol and stricter marine laws regarding the provision of sufficient lifeboats to carry all passengers.

The *Titanic* lay undisturbed on the ocean bed until 1985 when a team of US and French researchers located the wreck, lying 595 km (370 miles) off Newfoundland, by the use of new undersea robots equipped with TV cameras. Later dives showed that the liner had split in two as she sank.

Passengers lucky enough to escape in the lifeboats watched as the great ship sank, taking husbands, brothers, friends down with it.

The Attack on the *Lusitania* 1915

The sinking of the *Lusitania* by German torpedoes roused great anger both in Britain and America and was one of the reasons that America entered the war.

On 1 May 1915, Cunard's luxury liner *Lusitania* began her regular transatlantic crossing, carrying among her passengers many women travelling to join their soldier husbands. Since the outbreak of war the splendid 'floating hotel' had been under the direction of the Admiralty but had continued to make the Liverpool-Queensland-New York run every month.

The voyage was proceeding in spite of a warning issued a few days earlier by the Imperial German Embassy in Washington that the waters around the British Isles were considered a war zone and that 'vessels flying the flag of Great Britain, or any of her allies, are liable to destruction in these waters and that travellers sailing in the war zone on ships of Great Britain or her allies do so at their own risk.' However, the captain and crew were confident that the *Lusitania* would outrun any German U-boats and that, even if the ship was hit by a torpedo, she would probably stay afloat because of her system of watertight bulkheads.

The *Lusitania* sailed with 1,159 passengers, 702 crew and a cargo of furs, butter, cheese and canned goods. But in addition to these harmless items she carried 1,250 cases of shrapnel and 4,000 cases of cartridges stored next to the boiler room and listed on a supplementary manifest, signed after the ship had sailed and not seen by the captain.

Five days into the voyage, U-boat activity off Fastnet was reported and the captain took all the usual precautions, doubling the lookouts, closing as many watertight doors as possible and having the lifeboats swung out in case they were needed. As the liner sailed within a few miles of the Irish coast, it seemed impossible that there could be any real danger. Then at 14.10 on Friday, 7 May the passengers heard a dull thud – 'like the slam of a door' – as a torpedo fired by German U-20 struck the starboard side of the liner.

Immediately afterwards came a second major explosion, caused by the cargo, blowing up the boilers and tearing the heart out of the ship. Listing sharply to starboard, her engines disabled, the stricken liner swept round in a giant semi-circle. Though there were plenty of lifeboats to accommodate all those on board, the ship's steep list meant that many of them were impossible to launch. Boats on the port side needed to be pushed over the rail before they could be launched, but the frightened passengers crowded into them and refused to leave. As the crew tried frantically to free the boats, some fell to the decks, crushing people beneath them, others smashed into one another; one tipped its human load into the water where another boat crashed down onto their heads.

The U-boat crew, knowing that their single torpedo could not have destroyed the liner so completely, watched the chaos and terror through their periscope in amazed silence before turning for home. In less than 20 minutes the *Lusitania* had sunk. Only 663 of the 1,861 people on board survived.

'*Lusitania* torpedoed and sunk: world aghast at Germany's biggest crime' blared the newspaper headlines. An official statement from the German government that the *Lusitania* was carrying arms in her cargo did nothing to calm public fury on both sides of the Atlantic. The attack on the liner was one of the incidents that was to lead to America's entry into the First World War.

Fire on the Morro Castle 1934

In the early 1930s, Cuba was high on the list of holiday destinations for Americans and the two luxury liners, the *Morro Castle* and the *Oriente*, regularly made the run between New York and Havana. It was in September 1934, four years after her maiden voyage, that disaster overtook the *Morro Castle*, as she sailed up the New Jersey coast on her way home.

On the night of 7 September the captain, Robert Willmott, died suddenly from a heart attack. In the early hours of the next morning the night watchman saw smoke drifting from a ventilator and an officer sent to investigate found a fire already raging in the ship's library. Immediately the inadequacy of the fire fighting arrangements on board were revealed. The hydrants nearest the source of the fire, on the promenade deck, had been removed after a leak had caused a woman passenger to fall and bring a lawsuit against the owners. Valuable time was lost while crew ran to find hydrants from other decks. The acting captain, Chief Officer William Warms, proved unequal to the crisis; he failed to send out a prompt SOS and allowed the ship to steam full ahead into a strong wind that fanned the flames.

The crew were incompetent and untrained in their duties during an emergency and many thought only of themselves. The first six lifeboats, with a capacity of over 400 between them, later pulled into Spring Lake, New Jersey, carrying only 85 people, 80 of them members of the crew. Though the liner was only a few miles from the coast, 133 people died that night. Some suffocated in their cabins, others tried to squeeze through the portholes, but stuck tight and burned to death. The deck was crowded with men, women and children, some in their nightclothes while others, who had been at private parties, were in evening dress. As the heat of the decks became too hot for them to bear, they plunged into the sea, clinging to pieces of wreckage and screaming in terror.

The *Monarch of Bermuda*, answering the ship's SOS, arrived to find a horrifying sight. A passenger said later: 'The grimaces made by the people in agony at the portholes was something that I shall never forget. On the deck we saw a young fellow with his wife. She fainted in his arms and a huge tongue of flame popped out from the wall and sucked them in. We saw a man in pyjamas go up like a torch.'

By first light, a huge crowd of spectators had gathered on Asbury beach to witness the last hours of the burning ship as it drifted into the shore. Eventually the crowds became so great that squads of soldiers, armed with rifles, were rushed to the scene to control them.

In the subsequent enquiry, before a Federal Grand Jury, five officers were found guilty of negligence. A $13 million lawsuit was instituted against the owners, the New York and Cuba Mail Steamship Company of New York, by survivors and relatives of the dead; they claimed that the liner was badly designed and equipped, so that it was unsafe to sail as well as being undermanned and in the hands of incompetent officers.

The company eventually paid out $1¼ million in compensation. The cause of the fire was never established but most experts believed that it was the result of one carelessly dropped cigarette.

Below: Fire broke out on the *Morro Castle* in the early hours of a September morning and the flames spread quickly. **Right:** A young survivor is carried from the lifeboat to the waiting ambulance. Many passengers died trapped in the blaze.

The *Herald of Free Enterprise* Capsizes 1987

As passengers boarded the *Herald of Free Enterprise* at the Belgian port of Zeebrugge for the two and a half hour crossing back to Dover, England, many of them headed straight for the cafeteria. On 6 March 1987, well out of the holiday season, the ferry was only half full but there was a large contingent of day trippers, tempted by a cheap day excursion offer from P & O, the owners of the Townsend Thoreson line. Now, after a day's shopping, the trippers were hungry and thirsty. Also on board were 100 or so soldiers going home on leave from the British forces in Germany.

The ferry had completed her turning manoeuvre and was heading out of the harbour when she was seen to develop a sudden list – and a minute later, just outside the harbour wall, she keeled over. Only a shallow sandbank prevented her from turning over completely.

In the cafeteria and saloons, people were hurled on top of one another in a screaming, heaving mass. Some were unable to breathe, some were drowned as the icy water rushed in. All the lights went out and those still alive found themselves struggling in pitch darkness. Passengers below decks had little chance of survival. There was no time to lower lifeboats and though the crew threw lifejackets overboard to people who had been hurled into the water when the ship went over, many were already too numbed by the intense cold to put them on.

The starboard side of the ship was now uppermost and the crew worked manfully to haul up those they could reach on the port side. Some women found that they were pulled off the ropes by men desperate to save themselves

at all costs, but as well as stories of selfishness and cowardice, there were a number of examples of heroism. One passenger, 33 year old Andrew Parker, used his body as a human bridge over a 1.5 (5 ft) gap between a platform and a broken window which would lead to the safety of the starboard side. His 12-year-old daughter, his wife and several other passengers climbed over him, one at a time, and escaped.

Helicopters and a fleet of small boats worked constantly to scoop survivors out of the sea or lift them from the decks of the *Herald* but on shore there was confusion as survivors were landed in different places and taken to different hospitals. As there was no passenger list, they could make no accurate estimate of the number of survivors – or the number of dead.

Recovering the bodies was a long job; though divers working in darkness managed to recover most bodies from the upper decks, those on the lower decks had to remain where they were until several weeks later, when the *Herald* had been towed into the harbour and the thick layers of mud and silt had been pumped out.

The ferry was one of the roll-on/roll-off type type and in the past many experts had expressed doubts about the safety of this design, but their advice had been ignored. Initial enquiries showed that the ship had left her berth with the bow doors still open, allowing water to flood the open car decks. An inquest jury returned verdicts of unlawful killing on 187 victims and in June 1989 P and O European Ferries were charged with corporate manslaughter; seven individuals also faced manslaughter charges.

Right: The *Herald of Free Enterprise* keeled over just outside Zeebrugge. Below: Rescue workers search for the injured and the dead in the stricken ferry.

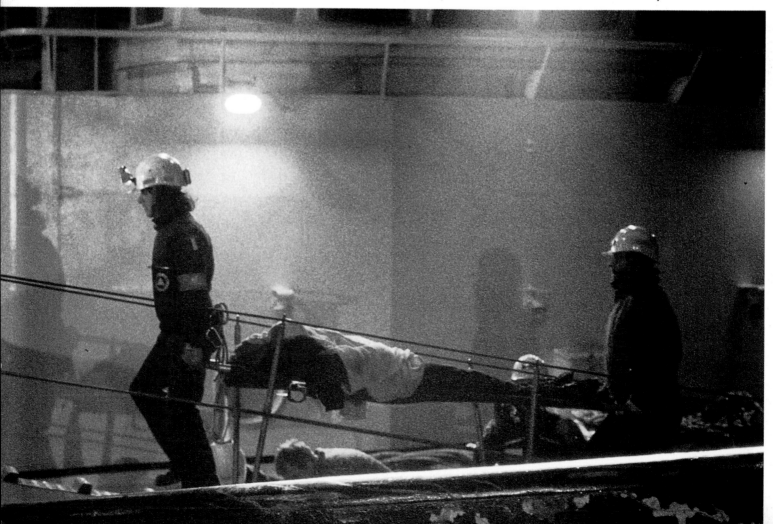

Air Disasters

The Death of the Airships R101 and the *Hindenburg*

The two airship tragedies of the 1930s, the first when the British R101 crashed in France while making its first flight and the second when German *Hindenburg* burst into flames as it was coming in to land, put an end to all the grand plans for fleets of passenger airships, cherished by countries all round the world. Until then, enthusiasm had been running high; between 1919 and 1930 airships had made seven successful crossings of the Atlantic, while more than half of the attempts at crossing by aircraft had resulted in failure.

The British government had moved seriously into the industry with the development of the R101 but progress was beset by political and technical difficulties. The five diesel engines weighed twice as much as the original estimate and no proper solution had been found to the problem of leaks from the 17 hydrogen-filled gas-bags by the time the airship set off on her much-publicized journey to Egypt via India with 54 people aboard.

As the ship crossed the French coast, the passengers had retired to bed after an excellent dinner, unaware that a tear had developed in the outer cover of the nose, rupturing the front gas-bags. The crew released ballast in the hope of levelling the ship and the engines were slowed but the R101 went into a dive and ploughed into a low hill near Beauvais. Only seven crew members survived the blaze that followed and Britain's involvement with the development of the airship was halted immediately.

The German airship industry continued, and its *Graf Zep-*

pelin had been flying successfully for several years when its sister ship, the *Hindenburg*, was completed in 1936. She was the largest airship ever built, with a length of 296 m (972 ft), and luxurious accommodation for 50 passengers. In the first year she safely covered more than 300,000 kilometres (186,000 miles) and there was no reason to think that the flight beginning on 3 May 1937 should be any different.

The *Hindenburg* set off from Frankfurt am Main to its US destination at Lakehurst, New Jersey, with a total of 97 passengers and crew on board. As it came in to land, a radio commentator, Herb Morrison, was on a routine assignment describing the scene when suddenly his voice took on a tinge of hysteria: 'It's broken into flames, it's flashing, flashing terribly, it's bursting into flames . . . this is one of the worst catastrophes in the world!' A few horrified minutes later he was sobbing openly. 'I'm going to step inside where I can't see it . . . I'm going to have to stop for a moment because I've lost my voice. This is the worst thing I've ever witnessed.' Amazingly, only 33 died in the holocaust.

Courts of enquiry were set up in Germany and the United States to discover the reason behind the explosion and many possibilities were discussed, including sabotage. The most likely explanation seems to have been a freak combination of circumstances. A build-up of hydrogen at the rear of the airship had been set alight by an electrical storm, ground electricity from which had been conducted along wet mooring ropes to the main framework of the ship. To complete the recipe for disaster, a layer of rain on the fabric of the envelope had converted the whole structure into one great electrical condenser.

Right: The wrecked skeleton of the R101 near Beauvais, as seen from the air. Below: The *Hindenburg* suddenly bursts into flames as it comes in to land.

THE ILLUSTRATED LONDON NEWS

REGISTERED AS A NEWSPAPER FOR TRANSMISSION IN THE UNITED KINGDOM AND TO CANADA AND NEWFOUNDLAND BY MAGAZINE POST.

SATURDAY, OCTOBER 11, 1930.

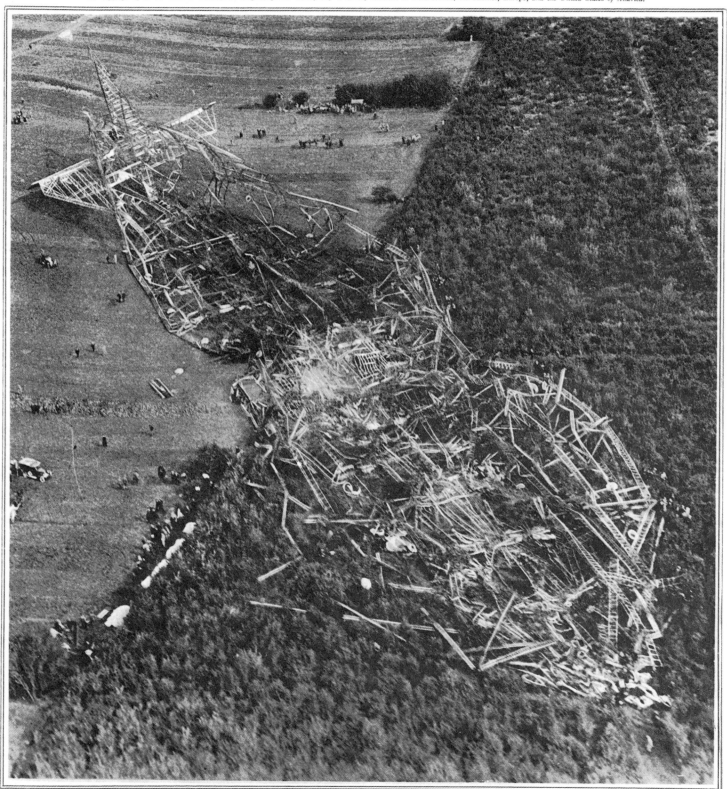

THE GREATEST DISASTER IN THE HISTORY OF AVIATION: THE TORN AND TWISTED SKELETON OF "R 101" AN AERIAL VIEW OF THE WRECK ON A HILLSIDE NEAR BEAUVAIS.

The destruction of the great British airship "R 101," which crashed in France at the outset of her projected flight to Egypt and India, in the early hours of Sunday, October 5, and was destroyed by fire, was a terrible blow to British aeronautics, more particularly in the loss of so many lives valuable to airship development. Here the wreck of the great airship is seen on a wooded hillside near the village of Allonne, a few miles south of Beauvais. The nose of the ship is seen among the trees in the foreground, and at the after-end is the framework of the rudders and elevators. Amidships, at the edge of the wood, are the burnt-out passenger quarters, whose distinguished occupants, including Lord Thomson and Sir Sefton Brancker, all perished. Detailed illustrations appear on later pages.

New York Mid-Air Collision 1960

Into the grey cold of a December morning in the Park Slope area of Brooklyn, New York, came the unbelievable; a flaming airliner crashed from the sky, demolishing a church, while its burning tailplane bowled down the street, filling the gutters with a blazing stream of jet fuel, setting cars on fire and spreading flames to nearby shops and offices.

The United Airlines DC8 jetliner had been approaching New York from Chicago, due to land at what is now Kennedy Airport at 10.45 on Friday, 16 December 1960 when it collided in mid-air with a Transworld Airlines Lockheed Super Constellation arriving from Columbus, Ohio, and due to land at La Guardia. The United Airlines plane had been carrying 84 passengers and crew; the Transworld plane, which crashed at one end of a small army/air force strip on Staten Island, had 45 people aboard.

The loss of life on the ground was remarkably small. On Staten Island the plane narrowly missed a group of houses and killed no one but those aboard. Once the fire was quenched, firemen pulled apart the wreckage with winches and crowbars and lifted out one body after another, covering them with army blankets provided by servicemen. A report that people had been seen falling from the plane as it came down sent coastguards searching the river and sea but, although they recovered six more bodies, all had died as they hit the water.

In Brooklyn children were already at school, offices and factories had started work and the cold, miserable weather had kept most people indoors so, in spite of the holocaust that followed in this densely populated area, only six people on the ground died. Moments after the crash hundreds poured out of the tenement buildings onto the street. One witness explained that any rescue work was impossible: 'the heat was terrific and the flames were shooting three storeys high. We couldn't get near the place . . . we heard no screams from the wreckage.' However, as firemen began their work, they discovered the sole survivor, an 11-year-old boy, Stephen Baltz, who managed to crawl out of the wreckage, his clothes on fire.

Stephen, who had been alone on the flight, travelling to spend Christmas with his mother, gave this first-hand account of the tragedy: 'I remember looking out of the plane window at the snow below covering the city. It looked like a picture out of a fairy book . . . Then, suddenly, there was an explosion. The plane started to fall and people started to scream. I held onto my seat and then the plane crashed. That's all I remember.' Though a medical team fought hard to save him, he died soon afterwards, his lungs destroyed by the intense heat of the fire.

The official enquiry, reporting in 1962, held the pilot and crew of the DC8 responsible for the collision; it had been 14.5 km (9 miles) off course and had failed to throttle back to the regulation speed required when flying at low level. By then, everyone realized how much greater the loss of life could have been: one section of the plane had narrowly missed a Roman Catholic school with 1,700 pupils as it plunged, flaming, to the ground, scattering debris in the school yard but injuring no one.

Above: In Brooklyn, pieces of the wrecked United Air Lines plane are loaded onto a truck. Left: Firemen sift through the wreckage on Staten Island.

The Tenerife Runway Crash 1977

A terrorist bomb exploded at Las Palmas airport on Gran Canaria on Sunday, 27 March 1977, and after warnings of a second bomb the airport was closed and flights were diverted to Los Rodeos airport on Tenerife. Among them were two Boeing 747s – Pan American flight 1736 bringing 373 holidaymakers from Los Angeles and New York to join a cruise ship, and KLM flight 4805 arriving from Holland with 234 passengers. Los Rodeos, a busy airport in its own right, was smaller and less well equipped than Las Palmas and the three air-traffic controllers on duty found themselves with 11 planes on the ground, all awaiting clearance for take-off. To add to the problems, a thickening mist was fast cutting visibility.

After several hours of waiting, both planes received clearance to taxi. Because of the congestion on the apron in front of the terminal, both planes were instructed to taxi up the main runway, in the reverse direction to normal. The plan was that the KLM flight should go to the end of the runway and turn ready for take-off while the Pam Am flight was to leave the runway at the third exit, though there was confusion over the instructions due to the controller's heavy Spanish accent. The exact reasons for what happened next may never be known but it seems that visibility was by now so bad that the American crew had ex-

treme difficulty in seeing the exits, with the result that they missed their turn and continued down the runway, unaware of their mistake.

While the control tower was still trying to check the position of the Pam Am jumbo, the Dutch plane was preparing for take-off and the two airliners ended up facing one another in the fog. Radio interference caused more confusion and the KLM captain, not realizing the true situation, thought that he had clearance for take-off. The Dutch jet was already travelling at 240 kmph (150 mph) when the Pan Am crew first saw it. The American captain tried to swerve in a last desperate attempt to avoid collision while the Dutch captain tried to lift the plane's nose to clear the other airliner.

The nose of the KLM Boeing just cleared the Pan Am plane but the engines and landing gear ripped through the fuselage. The Dutch airliner skidded back onto the runway, disintegrating and exploding, killing everyone on board. The 70 people who survived on the Pan Am flight were sitting at the front or on the left hand side, away from the impact. Some were hurled clear or leapt to safety; others were dragged from the wreckage by courageous survivors like Dorothy Kelly, a 35-year-old Pan Am purser from New Hampshire. Ignoring explosions from within the plane, she kept dragging out the dazed and injured until she could find no one else left alive; later she received a gallantry medal.

Controllers in the tower, hearing the explosions, first suspected that a terrorist bomb had blown up an airport fuel tank but when they tried to transmit warnings to the two jumbos, they were unable to make contact. By the time fire engines found their way through the foggy, crowded airport to the scene of the crash, they were met with the appalling sight of two blazing aircraft.

Below: A disabled airliner stands on the runway at Tenerife after the collision between two planes in bad visibility. Left: The grim job of sifting through the wreckage in search of bodies begins.

The Potomac River Tragedy 1982

Air Florida's flight 90 had been delayed by snowstorms at Washington D.C.'s National airport and finally took off, two hours late, only a few minutes after the airport re-opened in the afternoon of 13 January 1982. It was immediately obvious that something was badly wrong. As the plane juddered and shook, the captain was heard urging 'Come on, forward, forward, just barely climb.' 'Larry, we're going down!' exclaimed the first officer. 'I know it,' replied the captain.

Seconds after take-off the plane crashed into the Potomac Bridge, choked with rush hour commuter traffic, raking through several cars before it cannoned into the ice-covered river below. 'The plane seemed to hit the water intact in a combination of a sinking and ploughing action . . . I saw the cockpit go under the ice . . . I got the impression it was skimming under the ice and water,' said one of the hundreds of appalled onlookers.

Those in the nose of the plane died instantly as it plunged below the water. The main fuselage settled temporarily before it sank and commuters on the bridge could see the helpless passengers still strapped to their seats inside. From the tail, which floated for 20 minutes or so, people spilled into the water, so cold that none could survive for more than a few minutes.

It was impossible for emergency vehicles to react at full speed in a snowy rush hour and ambulances and fire engines were soon trapped in traffic jams, finding the wide pavements in front of the White House their only way through. As the rescue vehicles arrived and military helicopters whirred overhead, millions of families across the United States watched the events that followed live on their TV screens. They saw stewardess Kelly Duncan trying to catch one of the lifelines hanging from a helicopter but unable to hold on with her numbed fingers. She was rescued when a helicopter crew risked their lives, the pilot hovering almost at water level while his crewman climbed out onto the landing skids to haul her in to safety. Another young woman lost her hold on a lifebelt as she was being towed to shore and seemed doomed until 39-year-old office worker Lennie Skutnik plunged into the water, regardless of his own safety, and dragged her to shore; after his heroic rescue attempt he needed hospital treatment for hypothermia. Others were not so fortunate and there were horrifying stories of people still alive under the ice, watching rescue workers trying to break through but dying before they could manage it. There were only five survivors from the 74 passengers and crew of five, and there were five more victims among the motorists on the bridge.

It was a week before divers, working in the cold and dark, were able to recover the 'black box'. The evidence of the flight recordings was specially important in establishing the reasons for the crash, as poor visibility had prevented any of the airport control staff from seeing the 737 taking off. Investigators attributed the loss of the aircraft to failure to take adequate measures to deal with the exceptionally cold weather. Boeing 737s were known to be particularly vulnerable to icy conditions, and inclined to pitch and roll unexpectedly when their wings were icy, but the staff responsible for de-icing were not aware of the plane's special needs and the captain had underestimated the amount of ice on the wings.

Right: The Potomac bridge was jammed with traffic when the airliner hit. Below: On the left of the picture, a survivor struggles in the icy river.

The Korean 747 Shootdown 1983

Korean Airlines flight 007 was on a flight from New York to Seoul when it was reported missing. It had disappeared over Sakhalin Island, off Siberia, a highly sensitive Soviet strategic area, and first reports speculated that it might have been forced down by the Russians. The reality was far worse: the plane had been shot down by Soviet fighters with the loss of all 269 aboard.

The tape of transmissions by the Soviet interceptors told a grim story, as the pilot reported to controllers: 'I am closing on the target. Am in lock-on . . . I have executed the launch . . . The target is destroyed. I am breaking off the attack.' The Soviet authorities mounted a determined propaganda exercise, condemning the United States for 'deliberately planned provocations'. At a Moscow press conference, the chief of the Soviet general staff claimed that the 747 had been flying in restricted air space, without navigation lights and had ignored signals and warning shots. He maintained that the plane had been on a spying mission and that 'the aircraft's destruction and loss of life should be blamed on the US.'

The western world was stunned and horrified. The US Senate passed a resolution describing the shoot-down as a 'brutal massacre'. President Reagan called the action 'barbarous' and a world-wide 60-day ban was called on flights to the Soviet Union. The incident chilled relations between the super powers but within 12 months Moscow was admitting that the destruction of the plane had been a serious error and the United States no longer maintained that it had been a deliberate act of brutality.

The true story of what happened to Flight 007 remains a mystery. At the time of the incident, the airliner was more than 480 km (300 miles) off course, flying over an area known to be among the most sensitive in the world. The crew were apparently unaware of their true position as they passed over the Kamchatka peninsula with its missile testing sites. The first Soviet fighters were launched but they failed to intercept the Korean 747 and as it left Soviet air space they returned to their station. The 747 captain was still reporting his position, apparently believing that he was on course, as he headed for the southern tip of Sakhalin Island and for disaster.

No convincing explanation has been produced. It seems unlikely that the highly experienced flight crew of the 747 should have made crucial mistakes in programming the aircraft's complex Inertial Navigation System and then not noticed that things were going wrong. The claim by the Soviet authorities that the Korean airliner was carrying sophisticated electronic eavesdropping equipment seems unlikely, as this would have been difficult to conceal from mechanics servicing the aircraft at foreign airports. Equally unlikely was the suggestion that the violation of Soviet airspace was deliberately planned so that US intelligence could monitor the Russians' response, as the Russians had shown in the past that they would not hesitate to take tough action. Some sources suggested that the pilot might have been taking a short cut to save costs and deliberately relaying false positions but it seems inconceivable that he would take such risks for so little gain. As the voice and flight data recorders have never been recovered, we are unlikely to discover the answer.

In a demonstration against the shooting down of the Korean airliner, a member of the Korean-American Association sets fire to an effigy of the USSR.

The Lockerbie Crash 1988

Pan Am flight 103, leaving London Heathrow for New York three days before Christmas, was loaded with people going home for the holidays, or visiting family or friends over the festive season. At 9,450 m (31,000 ft) it suddenly disappeared from the radar screens, only two minutes after a routine exchange of information with air-traffic controllers. The plane had exploded over Lockerbie, a small market town of 3,000 inhabitants in the valley of the river Annan, in Scotland, killing all 259 passengers and crew on board.

Lockerbie residents heard a screeching sound, then a great bang that set the ground shuddering. Many saw a huge ball of flame hurtling down from the sky. One eyewitness, whose farmhouse was shaken violently, went to the window and saw a large dark shape in a distant field. Never dreaming that it was a plane he went to investigate. By the time he got there there was no smoke and no fire; only a large crater surrounded by mutilated bodies.

The four-ton engine, which had come down as a fireball, had missed houses in the most densely populated part of town and was buried 4.5 m (15 ft) deep. The forward section of the plane was found still ablaze 5 km (3 miles) east; a cabin door was found 30 km (18 miles) away. But part of the wings and the fuselage landed on houses in Sherwood Crescent, a quiet cul-de-sac, tearing through roofs and

The engine of the Pan Am plane came down as a fireball on the houses of Lockerbie and burning debris was scattered over a wide area.

walls. Dozens of cars exploded as they were hit by burning debris. Wreckage blocked the A47 trunk road running close to Lockerbie; great chunks of twisted metal fell in the streets and gardens and a great pall of smoke hung in the sky over the town.

At Kennedy Airport, dozens of people waited to meet their relatives and friends. Many were the parents of the 38 undergraduates from Syracuse University in upstate New York, who were returning home after a term of European studies in Britain. The first intimation that anything was wrong was a cryptic message on the arrivals board, shortly before the plane was due to land, telling them to contact ground staff. When they did so, they were taken to a lounge where staff broke the news that Pan Am flight 103 had crashed and that there were no survivors.

As the search for the dead began, Lockerbie town hall and the local ice rink were turned into temporary mortuaries. Some bodies had been found, still strapped to seats, near the centre of town; 20 were found in an area near the A74, 8 km (5 miles) to the south; another 60 were strewn across the local golf course. But many more were not found for days, and the relatives of the dead faced a long wait as a team of pathologists and orthodontists worked on the difficult task of identification, helped by dental records and fingerprints sent from the United States. It was not until five days later that the first bodies were taken away, driven through a guard of honour of Pan Am staff, police and soldiers, while more than 1,000 people lined the streets, many weeping openly.

Eleven people from Lockerbie died that night; all had their homes in Sherwood Crescent. At first 17 people were listed as missing but some were found alive and well, including an elderly couple who had staggered from their burning home onto the nearest main road and had been taken to hospital by a passing motorist. A 14-year-old boy survived because he was mending his bike at a friend's house, when his parents and sister died in their home. Immediately after the accident the townspeople took down their Christmas decorations and put many of their gaily wrapped presents away unopened – in a small town, everyone knew someone who was personally affected by the tragedy and they had no heart for celebrations. The local Church of Scotland minister voiced the feelings of many when he said: 'What can you do but weep?'.

From the first, the sudden disappearance of the plane from radar screens and the absence of a distress call from the pilot, coupled with the reliable record of the Boeing 747 aircraft, led the authorities to suspect sabotage. On 29 December Mr John Boyd, Chief Constable of Dumfries and Galloway, announced that a bomb was responsible for the disaster and that the investigation had now become 'a mammoth criminal enquiry of international dimensions'. As the flight had left 25 minutes late, it seemed safe to assume that the bomb had been intended to go off over the Atlantic, leaving no clues behind.

Searchers in helicopters, on foot and horseback combed the enormous Kielder Forest in Northumbria for telltale pieces of wreckage, though parts of the dense conifer proved impenetrable, without chopping down thousands of trees. More than 400 bags of personal possessions were gathered from the surrounding countryside; the sad collection included children's toys, clothes, letters, traveller's cheques and passports. Investigators interviewed everyone who had the slightest connection with the aircraft while it was on the ground at Heathrow, also with the connecting flight from Frankfurt. Six months after the crash, the saboteurs were still unknown.

Hundreds of relatives of the American passengers joined the people of Lockerbie for the memorial service at the Victorian parish church on 4 January 1989 when the town's traffic was at a standstill for an hour. The church held only 700, so the service was relayed in sound and TV pictures to several other halls, with seating for more than 1,000. Mourners heard the Rt Rev Professor James Whyte, Moderator of the General Assembly of the Church of Scotland, say: 'This was not a natural disaster such as an earthquake. Nor was it the result of human error or carelessness. This, we now know, was an act of human wickedness. That such carnage of the young and innocent should have been willed by men in cold and calculated evil is horror upon horror.'

Feelings on both sides of the Atlantic ran high when it was discovered that a warning of a bomb on a Pan Am jet had been phoned to the American Embassy in Helsinki on 5 December. The warning had been passed on to the Federal Aviation authorities who had informed American embassies but no public warning had been given. The US State Department pointed out that 87 phone threats had been received in the three months leading up to December 1988, almost all of them bogus.

Below: The homes in Lockerbie's Sherwood Crescent bore the brunt of the crash and 11 local people lost their lives. Right: Many tons of wreckage lay in the fields around the small Scottish town.

Rail Disasters

During the early years of steam trains, railroads gathered an aura of romance and adventure but it was soon obvious that any form of transport carries risks. The most spectacular of Britain's early accidents was the Tay Bridge disaster in December 1879 when the bridge over the 1.6 km (1 mile) long Tay estuary in Scotland, considered an engineering miracle at the time, collapsed in gale-force winds, catapulting a train and 76 passengers into the stormy waters below. There had already been worries about the bridge, which creaked and groaned in bad weather, but reinforcements were made and all was assumed to be well until the dark, windy night when the signalmen at the south end of the bridge watched a train begin its journey across the bridge only to lose sight of its lights completely when it was half way across. When they ran to investigate, they found that the central section of the bridge had gone, leaving rails dangling over the water. It was three days before the wrecked train was located and there were no survivors. Serious faults in the construction of the bridge were revealed later, including the fact that the bridge's inspector was unqualified and without experience.

One of the most famous of America's early rail disasters was commemorated in a ballad called 'The Chatsworth Wreck'; it was sung for years after six coaches from the Niagara Falls Special plunged into a ravine in 1887. A small wooden bridge near Chatsworth, Illinois, had caught fire after railroad employees had been burning weeds along the track earlier in the day. By the time the driver caught sight of the fire it was too late to stop. The first engine made it to safety but the bridge collapsed under the second engine which fell, along with the six following cars. Two more cars were derailed and in all 82 people died.

The worst train wreck recorded in the western world happened in Mondane, France, in December 1917, when a troop train, overloaded with 1,200 or more French troops returning from the Italian battlefields for Christmas leave, ran out of control. The engineer had complained about the overcrowding of the train, fearing it might prove too much for the old-fashioned handbrakes fitted on most of the cars, but he had been overruled and ordered to proceed. As the train descended a steep gradient, it gathered speed under the weight of the carriages and as it reached the sharp curve at the bottom, the first car shot off the track and cannoned into a wall; the rest of the carriages crashed into it. Fire broke out in the wrecked carriages and the ammunition carried by the troops began to explode. Over half of the soldiers died in the blaze but, because of wartime censorship, the death total has never been certain. The official total was 543, but many claimed that as many as 800 had died.

Britain had suffered her major troop train disaster two years earlier. On 22 May 1915 a train carrying 485 officers

Right: This engraving gives a dramatic picture of the rescue attempts following the collapse of the Tay Bridge. Below: A view of the bridge from the north, following the disaster.

and men of the 1st/7th Royal Scots met a local train head-on at Quintinshill in Scotland. The impact was heard miles away; the force of the collision was so great that the troop-train was reduced to a third of its original length. As the carriages caught fire a third train, this time an express, hurtled into the wreckage of the first coach. Instantly the train became a flaming mass fed by the gas cylinders beneath the carriages. Engines were heaped one on top of the other and carriages telescoped and overturned, trapping men beneath them. The carriage doors jammed and trapped passengers screamed in agony. Eight people died in the express and two in the local train, but in the roll-call of the Royal Scots regiment taken after the crash, only 52 men answered. From the remainder, 227 were dead and the rest injured, many of them seriously. The Board of Trade enquiry that followed found two signalmen responsible for the tragedy through their carelessness and lack of discipline. One was sentenced to three years in goal, the other received an 18-month sentence.

Over time, lessons have been learned from previous accidents and safety measures have improved but it is still possible for major accidents to occur, as the record of the past few decades has shown. Mexico has suffered more than one tragedy: in April 1955, 300 people died when their train plunged over a canyon near Guadalajara and in October 1972, a train crowded with pilgrims from the shrine of Catorce derailed on a fast downhill stretch and caught fire, killing 208 passengers.

Three trains were involved in an accident in Japan, near Mikawashima station, just outside the centre of Tokyo in May 1962. First a freight train collided with a commuter train then, as the injured and bemused passengers were scrambling out of the damaged cars, another commuter train ploughed into the wreckage. The lead car of the third train derailed, pulling four others after it and they rolled down a steep embankment, killing many of those who had jumped to safety after the first crash. More than 300 people were injured and 163 killed.

Below: Firemen fight the flames in the skeleton coaches of the Scottish troop train crash. Right: The triple train crash at a Tokyo station, seen from the air. On the right is the steam engine of the goods train; in the centre the passenger train and on the left the second electric train.

In June 1989, in the worst train disaster of recent years, 400 people, at least half of them children, died in central Russia when a gas pipeline exploded as two passenger trains, travelling in opposite directions, were about to pass each other. The explosion, in a ravine in the Ural mountains, derailed one train, sending it crashing into the other, which caught fire immediately. Wooden coaches crowded with passengers were burned out in less than 10 minutes, leaving helpless travellers with no chance of escape.

The trains were travelling to and from a popular Black Sea resort, carrying many whole families, as well as sick children on their way to recuperate at sanatoriums; the drivers were unaware of the rupture in the pipeline carrying gas from western Siberia to the industrial town of Ufa, leaking a highly explosive mixture within half a mile of the railway line. The aerodynamic effect of the two trains was such that it sucked up gas from the valley, then a spark from the wheels ignited it. The explosion was powerful enough to flatten trees within a 4.8 km (3 mile) radius, and windows in the nearest town, Asha, 11 km (7 miles) away, were blown out. Some of the carriages were left as lumps of twisted metal; several had melted in the heat of the explosion. Army units dragged burned bodies from the wreckage and searched the surrounding forests for more survivors while helicopters ferried the injured to hospital. Seven hundred injured were still being cared for a week after the crash.

Soviet leader Gorbachev, who flew to the crash scene, said that the accident – the worst train wreck in the history of the USSR – was caused by negligence. Gas had been escaping for some time, so that 'when the train passed by, a spark set off the explosion. It was real hell out there.'

Below: Military units and medical teams hurried to the scene of the explosion that wrecked two trains in the Soviet Union. Right: Wreckage and bodies were found scattered through the surrounding forest.

Fires and Explosions

Fires and explosions are some of the most terrifying of disasters – sudden, fierce, able to kill in minutes or leave survivors trapped in a confined space to perish more slowly. Strangely enough, one of the most famous fires in history, the Great Fire of London in 1666, cost only a handful of lives, while over 200 died in the Joelma Building in Brazil in 1974.

In a pit or oil-rig explosion, the victims may have no chance of escape, but the high death toll in a fire is often due to panic: in the terror-stricken rush for the exits in Chicago's Iroquois Theatre, twice as many were crushed or trampled to death as were killed by smoke and flames. Human carelessness and neglect plays a major role in such tragedies, too. Buildings turn into death-traps through lack of elementary precautions: firedoors firmly locked, no extinguishers or sprinklers, inoperable alarms, even unmarked exits. Hopefully, each tragedy has its own lessons for the future.

The Great Fire of London 1666

In the 17th century, London had a population of nearly half a million, most of them packed into decaying wooden houses in narrow streets, the upper storeys of the buildings overhanging so that they almost touched. When the fire began in a baker's shop in Pudding Lane in the early hours of Sunday, 2 September 1666, after a hot, dry summer, the whole street was ablaze so fast that the buckets of water rushed out by residents were useless.

When diarist Samuel Pepys heard that 300 houses had burned down by morning, he took a boat on the river to see for himself. 'Everybody endeavouring to remove their goods, and flinging into the river or bringing them into lighters that lay off; poor people staying in their houses as long as till the very fire touched them and then running into boats, or clambering from one pair of stairs by the water-side to another.'

As the fire raged on, attempts were made to stop it by pulling down buildings in its path but the work progressed too slowly and the flames, fanned by strong east winds, easily leapt the ruined buildings. By Monday night, the fiery red of the sky above London could be seen from 65 km (40 miles) away. In the city itself, the roar of the flames and the crashing of falling buildings mingled with the shrieks of terrified people. Many stored their valuables in St Paul's, thinking that its massive walls would protect it from the fire but it was to suffer the fate of so many other buildings, including the Royal Exchange and the Guildhall. Clergyman Dr Thomas Vincent described the destruction of the cathedral: 'now the Lead melts and runs down as if it has been snow before the sun; and the great beams and massy stones, with a great noise, fall upon the Pavement . . . now great flakes of stone scale, and peel off strangely from the side of the Walls.'

At last the winds dropped and, on Wednesday, the fire was brought under control, though 24 hours later the ground was still hot enough to scorch the shoes of those who went to view the damage. Four-fifths of London was in ruins and though only a handful of people died in the fire, hundreds of thousands had no roof over their heads. Most were camped out on the open spaces of Moorfields, the remnants of their possessions about them. King Charles II, who had been closely involved in the efforts to fight the fire, rode among them to reassure them that help was at hand and sure enough, within a week, all had found shelter in the homes of country people, or had erected temporary shelters on the ruins of their old homes.

Rebuilding plans were soon under way with Christopher Wren and other prominent architects submitting plans, most of them visualizing a city of wide avenues and open spaces, but the city had to be rebuilt as soon as possible, so none of them were adopted and instead reconstruction began on the basis of the old street plan. However, the new city was safer and healthier than the old, with brick or stone buildings instead of wood, and within the next few years work began on fifty new churches. Wren began work on the new St Paul's Cathedral in 1673 and his magnificent creation still dominates the City skyline. The Monument, a 61 m (200 ft) column of Portland stone, was erected in 1677, near the spot where the fire started.

Right: The 17th century painting by Waggoner shows the great fire, lighting up the Thames and the night sky. Inset above: Another representation of the flaming city by a Dutch painter.

The Iroquois Theatre 1903

Chicago's elegant new Iroquois Theatre was advertised as being 'absolutely fireproof'. Just how false those claims were was demonstrated tragically less than six weeks after its much-heralded opening, when fire killed over 600 people who had been attending a matinée on 30 December 1903.

In reality, the palatial theatre with its richly decorated interior was to become a death-trap. There were no chemical fire-extinguishers and no fire alarm, the sprinkler system was not in working order and the staff had no training in coping with an emergency. Though there were over 30 exits, most of them were locked and the theatre was far too crowded for safety. The pantomime *Mr Bluebeard*, which had had a successful run at London's Drury Lane theatre, was a big draw and while the theatre had 1,600 seats, there was evidence that the audience that afternoon totalled nearer 2,000, with hundreds standing, blocking the aisles and gangways.

In the middle of the performance, sparks from an overheated arc lamp ignited the gauze draperies used to create the effect of moonlight for one of the popular numbers. Fire spread quickly through the oil-painted canvas scenery on one side of the stage and up into the flies. Someone in the audience, seated near enough to see what was happening, shouted 'Fire' and people in the first few rows began to scramble into the aisles, but the band went on playing as stagehands began to lower the safety curtain. Backstage, performers and stagehands fled through an emergency exit. They were to be the lucky ones who escaped unhurt, but the draught created by the open door sent a great tongue of flame shooting under the partly lowered curtain and into the auditorium.

Utter panic followed. The lights went out as the audience fought to get to the exits. Many were mothers and children, school parties and groups of students, and as they piled up against locked exit doors, the smallest and weakest were soon trampled underfoot. Poor design meant that exits from the balcony and gallery led to a single passageway and scores died there in the crush. The fire escapes, which ran down into an alleyway alongside the theatre, were far too narrow for the numbers crowding into them and people fell by the dozen. Those who survived the fall did so because they fell on the heap of bodies already below.

The fire services arrived quickly and the flames were promptly extinguished with high-power hoses, but the damage had been done. Nearly 200 people had perished in the smoke and flames within 10 minutes of the start of the fire, some still sitting in their seats. Another 400 were killed in the panic-stricken stampede that followed. As the dead were laid out on the pavements, the marks of boots and shoes were etched into their faces and their clothes were torn from their bodies where others had tried to scramble over them where they fell. For almost three hours the rescue teams were bringing out two or three bodies from the theatre every minute.

Investigations following the fire showed up the many shortcomings of the theatre's safety precautions and the blame was passed to and fro. A coroner's jury found several people responsible but they were never brought to trial. However, the tragedy led to rigorous inspection of theatres up and down the country, and within the week 50 had been closed as unsafe. Stricter fire codes were introduced and penalties for infringement increased.

Below: The gutted interior of the Iroquois Theatre after the fire that claimed more than 600 lives. Right: A sketch from a magazine of the time, showing the panic inside the theatre as flames billowed out.

Seizième année. — Nº 780.

Huit pages : CINQ centimes

Dimanche 17 Janvier 1904.

Le Petit Parisien

SUPPLÉMENT LITTÉRAIRE ILLUSTRÉ

TOUS LES JOURS
Le Petit Parisien
(Six pages)
5 centimes

CHAQUE SEMAINE
LE SUPPLÉMENT LITTÉRAIRE
5 centimes

DIRECTION: 18, rue d'Enghien (10ᵉ), PARIS

ABONNEMENTS

PARIS ET DÉPARTEMENTS:
12 mois, 4 fr. 50. 6 mois, 2 fr 25
UNION POSTALE:
12 mois, 5 fr. 50. 6 mois, 3 fr

TERRIBLE CATASTROPHE A CHICAGO

INCENDIE DU THÉATRE IROQUOIS. — SIX CENTS VICTIMES

The Cocoanut Grove 1942

Saturday night was always a highspot at the Cocoanut Grove nightclub in Boston, Massachusetts. The crowd of regular local patrons was swelled by servicemen on weekend leave and, on the night of 28 November 1942, a large crowd of merrymakers was celebrating the victory of the Holy Cross football team in a match against Boston College. Though the club was licensed for only 460 people, no one tried to restrict the numbers and by 22.00 more than 1,000 people were crammed inside, drinking and dancing and making a deafening noise.

In such an atmosphere, it was impossible to tell exactly what caused the fatal fire. The blaze might have been started by a lighted match, tossed carelessly into the draperies, though some eyewitnesses reported seeing a sudden flash of fire, so perhaps the cause was an electric short circuit. The Hawaiian style decor of the lounge – the imitation palm trees, lacquered paper leaves twined from floor to ceiling, lights couched in coconut shells and imitation leather walls and seats – could hardly have provided better fuel for a fire and it spread with astonishing speed.

Journalist Martin Sheridan, who had been enjoying a night out at the club, described what happened: 'We had just been served with an oyster cocktail when, above the babble, I thought I heard cries of "fight" . . . I thought to myself it must be just a minor brawl . . . Suddenly someone at the end of our table screamed "fire!" Then I heard the loud crackling of flames . . . A cloud of black smoke surged across the room.'

If the club had been designed with safety in mind, all might have been well, as there were nine exits from the building, but most of them were heavily camouflaged by the Hawaiian decor. Unaware that there were several possible ways out, everyone tried to fight their way through the main revolving doors which were quickly jammed with bodies, some to be crushed to death within inches of safety. The windows of the club had been fitted with narrow metal frames and people who tried to squeeze through became wedged and were found later, many of them dead or dying. As hundreds of people surged towards one side of the room, part of the floor gave way, hurling dozens of people to their death in the basement. Others managed to climb down to the basement and shut themselves in the refrigerated storeroom where they remained, shivering but unharmed, until rescuers found them. One young Bostonian who found the way onto the roof and led 35 people to safety that way was hailed as a hero by the press.

The fire was extinguished within an hour and, as the bodies were carried out in a seemingly never-ending stream, every passing vehicle was commandeered as a makeshift ambulance to take the dead and injured to hospital. The immediate death toll was 433 and 59 more died of their injuries over the next few days.

Club owner Barney Welansky was sentenced to 12 years in jail. He had not obtained the necessary planning permission for the lounge where so many died; the electrical work was shoddy, carried out by unqualified people; there were no proper fire precautions in the building and, on top of all that, his insurance did not cover his patrons. Attention also turned on the lackadaisical attitude of the city authorities towards building regulations and safety precautions.

Firemen inspect the ruined shell of the Cocoanut Grove nightclub after the sudden blaze that killed nearly 500 revellers on a wartime Saturday night. The cause of the fire was never determined.

Mining Accidents

Mining has always been a hazardous occupation; men working in tunnels far below the ground are frighteningly vulnerable. Fire at a coal mine is a major threat to life, because once it ignites the inflammable methane gas given off naturally by the coal, the resulting explosion causes rockfalls or sends fire racing through the underground shafts.

In 1907, no less than 3,000 men died in the United States' coal mining industry. A freak accident caused over 360 deaths at Monongah, West Virginia. As the mine train carried out its load of coal, the end cars came uncoupled, gathering speed as they ran backwards on a gradient and crashing into electric cables, sending out a shower of sparks. As the coal dust caught fire an explosion shattered two adjacent mines. The damage was so extensive that it was several weeks before all the bodies were recovered. Though some had died in the fire, many had been crushed when the mineshaft caved in on top of them.

The tragedy of Cherry, Illinois, in 1909, began with a fire in bales of hay stored at the entrance to the mine. The flames spread quickly to the wooden supports of the tunnel. Four hundred men were working underground when the explosion came. Some managed to scramble out in time but most were trapped. The first group of rescuers hurried down immediately, but no sooner had the cage reached the bottom than the signal came to raise it again. By the time it reached the top, all the occupants were dead, overcome by methane fumes. It was 24 hours before the fire was under control and anyone could enter the mine to bring out the survivors – and the bodies. It was several days before the final count could be made: 259 men, including several of the would-be rescuers, had lost their lives. Several of those trapped below had been so badly injured that they were shot by one of their colleagues to end their intolerable suffering.

Of the 960 men working underground in the mine at Senghenydd, near Cardiff in Wales, 439 died after an explosion on 14 October 1913. Children on their way to school and housewives clearing up after breakfast heard

Clouds of smoke rise from the Llewellyn Portal of the coal mine near Manninton, West Virginia, where 78 miners were trapped underground.

the muffled explosion and ran to the pit, where they saw a thick cloud of smoke pouring from the shaft. They stood silent, hour after hour, as rescue teams from all over the Welsh valleys battled with flames and foul air to bring out those who were still alive. Hope surged anew when 18 men were found alive, 16 hours after the explosion, but they were to be the last. After 6 days, 400 men were still unaccounted for and presumed dead. There were few families among the pit community who were not in mourning for one or more of their men. One woman lost her husband, four sons and three brothers in that single accident.

Another Welsh pit, the Gresford Colliery near Wrexham, had to be sealed for seven months following several major explosions in September 1934. Though rescuers made several attempts to penetrate the barrier of raging fire, they had to abandon their attempts late the following day. The authorities declared: 'that no person can possibly be alive in the workings. In these circumstances and in view of the increasingly grave risk to the men engaged in combating the fire . . . it would not be right to continue to expose workers to such a serious risk.' The sealed mine became a tomb for 264 men.

When a series of explosions in the early hours of the morning led to fierce underground fires in the mine at Mannington, West Virginia on 20 November 1968, no one knew exactly how many men were trapped below in the 183 m (600 ft) shaft; one of the effects of the explosion was to blow out the office where the records were kept. Mine officials had to check with the homes of every miner on the night shift: the final list showed 21 men were safe, but 78 were unaccounted for. The initial explosion came at 05.40 and three other blasts followed, with a column of smoke several hundred feet high pouring from one of the entrances. Rescue teams, unable to enter the mine for fear of more explosions, worked to re-direct the air flow in the hope of preventing the spread of the fire so that miners would have a chance to get to safety in other parts of the pit. Nearly 40 hours after the first blast came another, sending flames shooting so high into the air that the fiery glow could be seen from towns many miles away.

There were more explosions and with each one, hope dwindled for the men. Only two ventilation fans were still working to provide air to the sections of the mine where men could have taken refuge from the fire, though the heat and lethal fumes made their survival unlikely. Any air in the mine would help to keep the fire burning – no air meant that any survivors would suffocate. When tests showed that fire had reached the last of the underground areas where the men might have taken refuge, even recovery of the bodies was deemed impossible and the mine was sealed on 30 November.

In Kellogg, Idaho, miners worked to bring up silver, not coal; the huge mine is one of the deepest and richest silver mines in the United States. Working here was always diffi-

Tom Wilkenson, one of the miners who survived for a week in the lower shafts of the Kellogg mine after the fire, is brought to the surface on 9 May 1972.

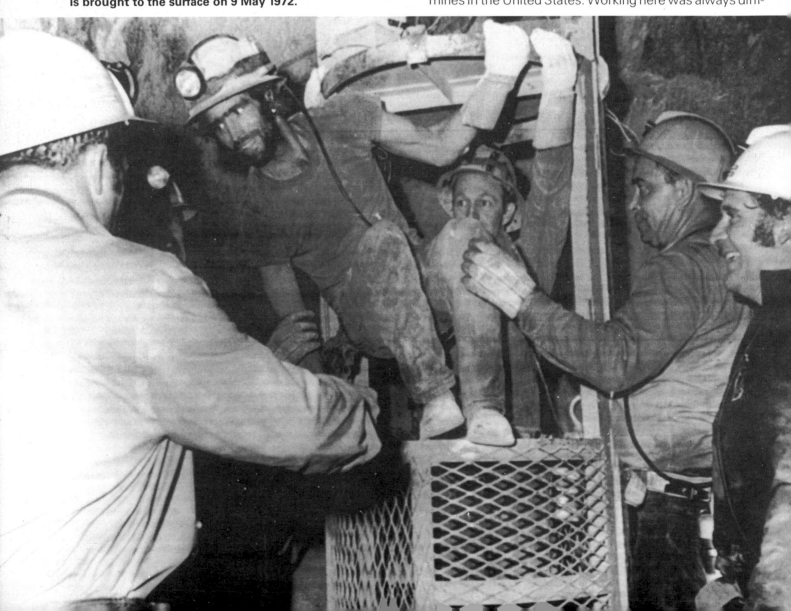

cult, with the temperature in the mine often so high that men could only work for 30 minutes at a time, but the rewards were high enough to persuade miners to put up with all the difficulties and dangers. It was probably the intense heat that led to the tragedy of 2 May 1972, when a fire started deep in the mine, in an area no longer in use; later, enquiries concluded that the cause was probably spontaneous combustion in old timber. Thick smoke penetrated the main ventilation shafts and while rescuers

in special masks sealed off empty shafts and brought up some survivors, others pumped oxygen into the lower levels of the mine, hoping to help the several dozen men known to be somewhere below. After a week, 47 bodies had been recovered and hopes were fading for the remainder of the missing miners, when two men were found 1,465 m (4,800 ft) down. They had been with seven others who ran for the lower shafts, out of reach of flames and fumes, but the other five had been overcome by carbon monoxide on the way. The fresh air being pumped into the shaft had kept them going, but there were no more miracles: the following day the last of the 91 bodies were brought out.

The Sunshine silver mine in Kellogg, Idaho, seen from the air soon after the fire that broke out deep within the mine, in a shaft no longer in use.

The Joelma Building 1974

The conditions existing in Brazil's largest city, São Paulo, in the 1970s added up to a major fire disaster waiting to happen. The city was growing fast, at the rate of at least 1,000 new residents every day. More than 400 new buildings were completed every week, many of them skyscrapers. They were erected with little or no attention to fire hazards, usually without essential precautions such as fireproof floors and insulated emergency stairways. In a population of 8,000,000, the city employed only 1,300 firefighters, but even if their numbers had been far greater, their ladders and hoses could not have reached the upper floors of high-rise buildings.

On the morning of 1 February 1974, 650 people were working in one of the city's newest office blocks, the Joelma Building, when fire broke out on the 11th floor of the building and spread quickly upwards, fuelled by the inflammable plastic used widely in the interior decoration. The first six floors were taken up by a car park and immediately above were the offices of the Crefisul Bank. Most of the people below the 11th floor escaped unharmed but for those caught above the fire – and beyond the reach of the firemen's hoses – it was a different story.

The fire struck so swiftly that a porter on the 10th floor only realized what was happening when he saw people streaming down the stairs: 'I saw women stripping off their clothing and everybody was shoving like mad to get down. When someone fell down, the mob trampled over him; I saw a young girl trampled to death. On the 11th floor I saw people run through a barrier of fire with their hair and clothing in flames. Others just stood there petrified and did not move until the flames swallowed them up.'

Television cameras arrived and crowds of sightseers blocked the road, delaying rescue services as they tried to get to the scene. The firemen's ability to help was strictly limited and they had to watch helplessly as some of the trapped people decided that jumping to their death was preferable to waiting for the flames to reach them. One or two yelled out last messages as they fell. A few lucky survivors were carried on the backs of rescuers who had fired ropes, harpoon-like, from neighbouring buildings and crawled across to collect them one by one.

Those watching below could see through the smoke to the flat roof where scores of people ran backwards and forwards, vainly seeking a way to safety and screaming for help. Helicopters hovered overhead, but the heat was too intense to allow them to land and the pilots had to stay well above the building to prevent their fuel tanks from exploding. Hours later, when the fire was eventually brought under control, they were able to bring the helicopters onto the flat roof and pick up the 80 or so people who had managed to survive the smoke and flames.

Temperatures inside the building had been so high that many of the bodies were reduced to ashes, and identification was slow, so it was some time later that the official death count of 227 was confirmed. The cause was never discovered. One strong possibility was an overheated air conditioning vent, but a charred tin of paint-thinning fluid, found by firemen near the original seat of the fire, might suggest arson. The city's fire chief was dismissed, as a scapegoat, but the deeper fault lay with the city authorities who were more interested in the city's quickly earned prosperity than in safety rules and regulations.

Below: As flames roar from the Joelma building, rescue workers bring out those trapped in offices on the upper floors. Inset left: A man, trapped by the fire, jumps to his death from the high-rise building. Over 200 perished in the disaster.

The MGM Grand Hotel 1980

The MGM Grand Hotel on the famous Las Vegas Strip, which tempts gamblers for high stakes from all over the world, was opened with a great fanfare in 1973. The multi-million dollar Grand Hotel was 26 storeys high, with five restaurants and one of the largest casinos in the world; top stars like Tom Jones and Engelbert Humperdinck earned $200,000 a week entertaining in cabaret.

Seven years later this glittering pleasure palace was to be the scene of one of the worst fires in the history of the United States. At 07.15 on 21 November 1980, cooking fat in the basement kitchen caught fire and within seconds turned into a huge fireball, erupting into a casino crowded with gamblers playing the tables and slot machines. Some were engulfed immediately, most fled as the flames fed hungrily on the thick carpets and plastic furnishings and a huge electronic keno board, used for a bingo-style betting game, exploded.

The fire alarms failed to work, their circuitry burned out before they could sound and there were no smoke detectors in the bedrooms, so the first warning most of the 1,000 or so overnight guests had of the fire was the noise of fire engines and ambulances racing to the scene. A couple from Michigan heard nothing from the 22nd floor and were horrified to hear the news when they turned on their radio. They put mattresses against the walls, blocked the opening under the door with towels – and prayed until rescuers came.

Some guests died, overcome by smoke and the fumes from synthetic furnishings before they could think about saving themselves. People trapped in the upper storeys broke windows and screamed for help, even beginning a perilous climb down the side of the building. Police with loud-hailers told them to stay where they were and wait for rescue, but it was soon obvious that firemen's ladders could not reach beyond the ninth floor. Workmen on an adjoining building site improvised scaffolding and some managed to scramble to safety. Many more were winched up from the roof by US Air Force helicopters.

Outside, shocked survivors milled about in the carpark, some in night clothes, some in full evening dress, searching for friends and relatives among the injured as they waited for ambulances to take them to hospital. In the two hours it took to get the fire under control, rescue workers plunged back again and again into the blazing building saving guests from rooms, from lifts and staircases where they were trying to batter down locked fire doors. One team found 18 dead on one staircase, overcome by smoke and fumes before they could open a jammed door.

Eighty-four people died in the fire and 600 more were injured. Lawsuits amounting to nearly $2 billion were filed against the MGM Hotel Corporation. There was widespread criticism of the safety standards at the hotel, including the lack of smoke detectors and sprinklers, but the hotel had been built according to the fire code existing at the time. A far stricter code had been introduced in 1979,

Above: Helicopters were used to winch many of the trapped guests to safety from the burning hotel. Below right: The famous Las Vegas hotel made a spectacular setting for one of the worst fires in the history of the United States.

but buildings completed before that date did not have to comply. In 1981 MGM opened their new $25,000,000 hotel, equipped with the very latest in computerized fire detection systems, claiming that it was now 'one of the safest high-rise hotels anywhere in the world.'

The Australian Bush Fires 1983

Bush fires are a constant hazard in the hot, dry summers of Southern Australia. The older generation of bush dwellers, accustomed to a peaceful existence in communities 200-300 strong, remember 'Black Friday', when bush fires in Victoria killed 71 people. The holocaust that raged on Ash Wednesday, 16 February 1983, in South Australia and Victoria was to rival anything the local 'bush brigades' of firefighters had ever faced before.

Temperatures through the summer had reached record heights, exacerbating the effects of the three-year-long drought in the outback. Daily warnings about fire hazards were broadcast as the bush (the scrub and grassland areas between outback and the urban centres) became so dry that a single spark could lead to an instant conflagration.

Fires apparently started in several places at almost the same time, in the afternoon of a sizzling day when temperatures had reached 43°C (110°F). Three began outside Adelaide, four outside Melbourne, where the eucalyptus trees of the area burned greedily, their oil-filled leaves turning into fireballs. By the time the fire bore down on Cockatoo, a little town east of Melbourne, the fireballs were 12 m (40 ft) high and the residents saw them racing towards them like huge golden globes. Some tried to flee by car but by now the fire was tearing along at up to 160 km an hour (100 mph) and they were soon swallowed up. Twenty-nine people died at Cockatoo but among the survivors were a family who hid inside a water tank at their hillside home, crouching in water that rose almost to boiling point as the fire raged outside. In the brick-built schoolhouse, 120 children sheltered under wet blankets while firefighters, risking their own lives, playing hoses on the roof.

The fire services, with the help of hundreds of volunteers, worked day and night without a break, but 12 firemen died at Mount Gambier, trying to fight a raging inferno with only two water tankers at their disposal. Seaside hamlets disappeared in the flames. Those with cliff-top homes at Lorne and Angleseay fled to the beaches, remaining marooned overnight as their houses blazed above them. The fire came far too near to Melbourne for comfort. As the flames rose above ridges 32 km (20 miles) away, bulldozers and excavators stood ready to dig vast fire trenches to halt its advance.

It was 48 hours before the fire was fully under control and the causes were never known for certain. Many suspected arson, insisting that sheer carelessness, like a dropped cigarette, could not explain several fires starting simultaneously. Another theory was that strong winds had snapped overhead powerlines that would quickly set fire to the inflammable eucalyptus trees. Whatever the cause,

the damage done by the fires was only too obvious. More than 8,500 people were homeless, many of them unable to salvage any possessions from the heaps of charred timber where their homes had been. Scores of fruit growers and dairy farmers were bankrupted, more than 200,000 sheep and cattle were lost and 61,000 hectares (150,000 acres) of farm and forest land were devastated. Worst of all, more than 70 people lost their lives.

Right: A bush fire rages with terrifying force near Barlee Range in North West Australia. Inset above: A fireman bravely tackles a blaze caused by a spark igniting tinder dry ground.

The Piper Alpha Explosion 1988

Only 62 men out of 228 survived the explosions that ripped through the Piper Alpha oil rig platform in the North Sea. Most of those who escaped were working on deck at the time and were able to jump into the sea, but their colleagues who were resting in the multi-storey accommodation block, demolished when a gas leak below set off two huge blasts, had no chance.

Piper Alpha was a 34,000 ton platform opened in 1973 and operated by the US corporation, Occidental Petroleum. Normally it produced 167,000 barrels a day and was operated by a crew of 200, working in 12-hour shifts. At the time of the accident there were more workers than usual on the rig, carrying out development work. The first explosion came at 21.30 on 6 July 1988, shortly after the workers had heard the squealing of escaped gas 'screaming like a banshee', and within minutes the rig was ablaze from top to bottom, the flames rising 120 m (400 ft) in the air.

From the support vessel *Thorus*, which picked up survivors, some so badly burned that the skin was peeling from their bodies, men could be seen waving frantically from the rig in the minutes after the first explosion, before the second 'just blew them away'. For an instant, bodies could be seen silhouetted against the flames. Three men had climbed up the gantry at the very top of the platform to escape the fire, but there was no escaping the blast and they were never seen again. 'It was just as though the platform had been blown up by an atomic bomb,' said one man. 'There was a vast mushroom cloud above it and flames shooting into the air.'

Survivors were to tell horrific tales of finding themselves surrounded by metal so hot that it was melting, feeling their skin blistering as they tried to keep their footing on the tilting platform. Men trapped in the galley were yelling into their radios: 'What's happening? Is anyone getting out? We're going to die in here.' Those who managed to get on deck had to choose between certain death in the flames and possible death in the icy seas. As they struggled in the water, weighed down by their heavy working clothes, debris crashed into the sea around them.

The immense heat from the blazing rig hampered rescue operations and huge bubbles of gas kept bursting up from the pipes below and igniting as they reached the surface. The world's most famous oil troubleshooter, Red Adair, was flown in to cap the flow of oil and gas that was fuelling the flames, but his team was beaten back by heavy seas and high winds and it was days before the fire could be brought under control.

A year later, relatives of the victims sailed to the site of Piper Alpha, 120 miles northeast of Aberdeen, in Scotland, to cast flowers on the water and hear prayers read by a Church of Scotland minister. On the same day North Sea oil workers staged a 24-hour strike, claiming that many of the faults that caused the Piper Alpha tragedy still existed and that the oil companies had been too slow to invest the

Above: A massive explosion wrecked the Piper Alpha oil rig, in its lonely position in the inhospitable North Sea. Right: Those who saw the rig ablaze said that it looked as though a bomb had struck it.

necessary money to make the radical changes needed in platform design, so that work on the rigs would be safer in the future.

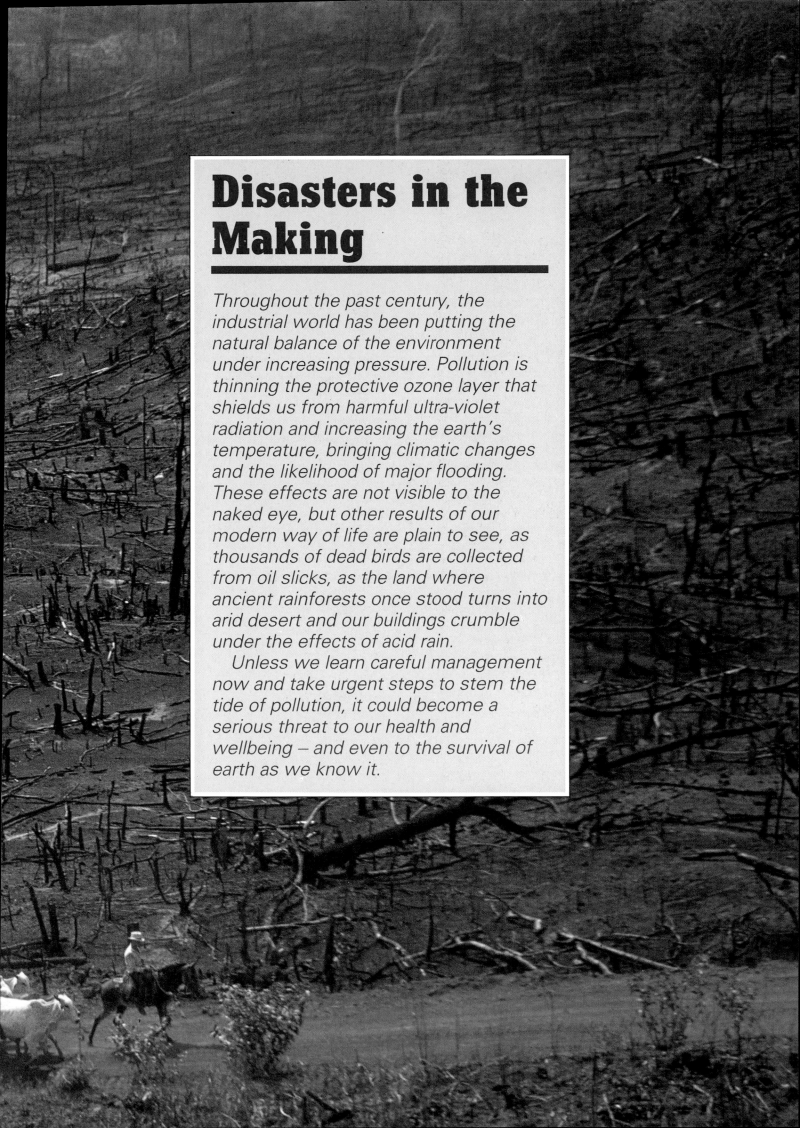

Disasters in the Making

Throughout the past century, the industrial world has been putting the natural balance of the environment under increasing pressure. Pollution is thinning the protective ozone layer that shields us from harmful ultra-violet radiation and increasing the earth's temperature, bringing climatic changes and the likelihood of major flooding. These effects are not visible to the naked eye, but other results of our modern way of life are plain to see, as thousands of dead birds are collected from oil slicks, as the land where ancient rainforests once stood turns into arid desert and our buildings crumble under the effects of acid rain.

Unless we learn careful management now and take urgent steps to stem the tide of pollution, it could become a serious threat to our health and wellbeing – and even to the survival of earth as we know it.

The Ozone Layer

In the late 1960s, scientists began voicing concern over the possible depletion of the ozone layer, the region in the earth's stratosphere that absorbs the sun's ultra-violet radiation and acts as a filter, protecting us from its harmful effects. In the last 20 years the world's ozone layer has thinned by 3 per cent, but the really dramatic findings came in 1987 when the Antarctic Airborne Ozone Experiment found a hole in the ozone layer over Antarctica in the spring, where the layer was reduced to 40 per cent of the pre-1975 level and at one place to 97 per cent. Recent investigations suggest that a similar process has taken place in the Arctic.

The major culprits in the destruction of the ozone layer have been identified as chlorofluorocarbons, or CFCs. They were invented in 1930 as a coolant for fridges and their useful properties – they are non-toxic, they do not burn or react with other chemicals – led to their widespread use in aerosols, plastic foam, fridges and air conditioners. Once CFCs are released into the air they gradually rise into the stratosphere, where ultraviolet decomposes them and releases free chlorine, which works to destroy the ozone. The hole appears above Antarctica because of special climatic conditions which produce a vortex of air, trapping chlorine monoxide during the severe winter freeze. The chlorine is then released by ultra-violet rays as the spring brings back the sun, with consequent destruction of the ozone layer. Inside the ozone hole, levels of chlorine monoxide were found to be 100-150 times above normal.

As the ozone layer thins, we are exposed to more ultra-violet radiation which, as well as causing sunburn and ageing the skin, can cause skin cancer. According to the US Environmental Protection Agency, a 1 per cent reduction in the ozone layer would mean 70,000 extra cases of non-malignant skin cancer throughout the world. The malignant form of skin cancer, melanoma, which currently causes 10,000 cases a year, would increase by 1-2 per cent for every 1 per cent of ozone lost. Certain types of crops including cabbages, soya beans and peas are vulnerable to ultra-violet radiation, which can also penetrate below the surface of the sea and destroy the algae which are essential for the survival of marine life.

Some governments acted early to limit the damage: in 1978 the US government banned the use of CFCs in aerosols, except for some essential uses, and some Scandinavian countries followed suit. In September 1987 the Montreal Protocol, signed by 62 governments, came into force and the signatories committed themselves to halving their output of CFCs by 1999. Since then, the EEC has agreed in principle to an 85 per cent reduction. Many scientists argue that this is too little and too late and that, as CFCs remain in the atmosphere for several decades, the damage is already irreversible. Others argue that the harmful effects of ozone depletion have been vastly exaggerated. They point out that if the ozone layer disappeared completely over the temperate zones, the intensity of ultra-violet radiation would only be as intense as that currently experienced in the tropics. In 1895, they say, the eruption of Krakatoa destroyed nearly one third of the ozone layer without catastrophic results.

Below: Satellite map of the ozone 'hole' (the blue region) over Antarctica (outlined in black). First seen in 1980, the 'hole' has grown every year. The map was made on the UN Nimbus 7 Weather satellite. Right: Research balloons being prepared for launching into the stratosphere. They carry instruments designed to measure the composition of the upper atmosphere, adding to our knowledge of how man-made chemicals are depleting the ozone layer.

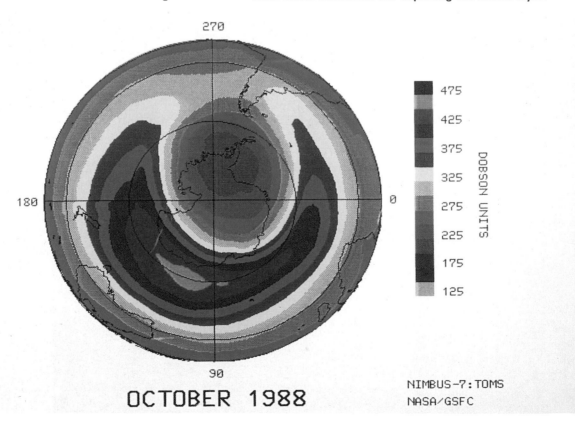

270

180   0

90

OCTOBER 1988

DOBSON UNITS

475
425
375
325
275
225
175
125

NIMBUS-7:TOMS
NASA/GSFC

The Greenhouse Effect

In the 21st century we shall be living in a warmer world and predictions of the likely average temperature rise range between 1.5° and 4.5°C (34.7° and 40.1°F). This global warming is caused by the 'greenhouse effect', in which certain gases trap the sun's heat, rather like the glass of a garden greenhouse. These gases, chief among them carbon dioxide, let solar radiation through to warm the earth's surface; the warm surface then radiates heat back into space but the 'greenhouse gases' block this radiation and re-cycle the heat, instead of allowing it to disperse. As the earth's temperature rises, more water evaporates from seas, lakes and rivers and the water vapour absorbs radiation even more easily than the gases, so the warming effect increases.

In recent times, the amount of greenhouse gases – about 40 are already known, though many more may be identified in the future – has been increasing rapidly. The most important is carbon dioxide, which accounts for about half the greenhouse effect. We produce more than 5 billion tons of carbon dioxide every year, primarily from burning fossil fuels. The vast majority of this comes from the industrialized world, with the United States contributing 24 per cent. Britain contributes 3 per cent, which is higher than most EEC countries. The destruction of forests also contributes to the increase of carbon dioxide in the atmosphere (see Deforestation page 186). In the 18th century the air contained around 265 parts per million by volume (ppmv). In 1958 this had risen to 315 ppmv and in the following 30 years it rose to about 350 ppmv.

Methane, or marsh gas, is the next in order of importance and levels rose by 1 per cent a year during the 1980s. Methane is produced in swamps and marshes and the guts of animals. The world's rice paddies probably account for 30 per cent of methane production and the doubling of the number of cattle over the past 40 years has made a substantial contribution. Modern methods of refuse disposal, with vast amounts of organic materials pressed down into the smallest possible space, lead to the production of large amounts of methane, and development in the Third World is likely to lead to substantial increases.

Nitrous oxide, produced naturally and by man, is increasing more slowly, at about 0.2 per cent a year, and the prime offenders are power stations and vehicle exhausts. Other greenhouse gases are chlorofluorocarbons (see The Ozone Layer page 176) and low-level ozone, created by the action of sunlight on hydrocarbon, and nitrogen oxides emitted by car exhausts, which produce a photochemical smog in cities like Los Angeles and Mexico City.

No one is certain what changes the greenhouse effect will produce on regional climates but they could be dramatic. The temperate zones may experience more extreme weather conditions than before, with more droughts, storms and floods. Some climatologists believe that dramatic weather like America's fierce drought in 1988, the surprise floods in Africa and India in the same year and the British hurricane in October 1987 are harbingers of the global warming process but so far, this is only a theory.

Climatic changes are unpredictable; for instance as the

Below: Smog contributes to global warming with the production of ozone, one of the greenhouse gases. Right: Paddy fields are important to the economy of many countries, but they produce nearly one third of the world's methane.

lakes and rivers evaporate, the resulting water vapour might be carried long distances before it turns to cloud and rain over mountains or sea, so that countries like Britain could become wetter while most of North America becomes drier. Regions with hostile climates at the moment might take over from today's fertile areas as the bountiful crop producers of the future, and this could bring far-reaching political and economic consequences. While temperature rises could give a great boost to agriculture in northern Europe, its effects on water-deprived southern Europe could be very severe. In the United States, it would probably be good news for the north and west, but could mean catastrophe for the east and south.

As the world warms, glaciers will melt and seas will expand, increasing their volume and flooding low-lying land. The extent of the changes in both climate and sea levels depends, of course, on the level of temperature rises. In 1984 the US Environmental Protection Agency predicted average rises of 2°C (3.6°F) by the middle of the next century and 5°C (9°F) by 2100. The US Research Council gave much the same estimates but thought it would take 25 years longer.

Once again, estimates vary widely but the greenhouse effect could cause the seas to rise anything between 20 cm (8 inches) and 6 metres (20 ft). A 1 metre (3 ft) rise would destroy 4,500 square kilometres (1,737 square miles) of Egypt's farmland and make over 5,000,000 people homeless, as well as flooding most of Bangladesh. A 6 metre (20 ft) rise would mean that many of the world's major cities, including New York, London, Peking, Sidney and Bangkok would all disappear under water. The great fear is that if the earth warms by 4°C (39.2°F) or more, the polar ice caps, which contain 98 per cent of the earth's fresh water, might melt. In the past few years observers have noticed that the number of huge icebergs breaking loose from the Antarctic – the giants can be as big as 6,000 square kilometres (2,316 square miles) – have increased. A complete melt of the polar ice caps would mean a rise of 50 metres (165 ft), with devastating effects.

Many scientists believe that if the planet is to be saved from catastrophe, immediate and far-ranging action must be taken, but the problems are immense. Keeping global warming down to 0.1°C (32.18°F) or less per decade, a temperature rise that would allow countries to adapt within a reasonable timescale, would mean cutting total carbon dioxide emissions by 50 per cent. Some of this could be achieved by switching from coal to oil or natural gas, both producing less carbon dioxide, but there would be political difficulties in countries where coal is a major industry. Nuclear power might help to reduce the carbon dioxide in the atmosphere, but would bring other disadvantages and dangers. Renewable forms of energy, including wind, wave and solar power, could be exploited but governments tend to be more concerned with the current balance sheet than with temperatures in the next century. In Canada the budget for renewable energy research was cut by half between 1984 and 1988, and at roughly the same time the United States cut its budget for solar energy research by two thirds.

Cutting down the overall amount of energy used would take wholehearted international effort, as plans for the increasing use of energy in developing countries are likely to cancel out any energy saving accomplished by the industrialized nations. Efforts on the part of prosperous countries towards such agreements lay them open to accusations of trying to prevent those in the Third World from enjoying a better standard of living.

Below: Air pollution over Rome; car exhausts and industrial emissions fill the air above many of our major cities with hazy smog. Right: The power stations are among the major culprits.

Acid Rain

In 1986 the British government was at last obliged to acknowledge the link between sulphur dioxide pollution from her power stations and the death of fish in Scandinavian lakes, and the United States government, after years of denial, admitted that US pollution was having a devastating effect on lakes in Canada. The cause is acid rain, invisible but highly damaging. Its main components are sulphur dioxide, produced by the burning of fossil fuels, mainly in power stations, and nitrogen oxide, mainly from vehicle exhaust emissions, with power stations contributing. Every year, man pumps 100,000,000 tons of sulphur into the atmosphere from the burning of fossil fuels and in 1970 the United States alone was producing 32,000,000 tons. Sulphur dioxide is often carried for long distances before it falls to earth as acid rain, hence the disasters faced by Norway, Sweden and Canada. Though these countries have instituted their own stringent pollution controls, they cannot solve the problem themselves, as much of their pollution is imported from other countries.

Acid rain has existed for 150 years, as long as coal has been burned on a large scale to produce power, and over the past 40 years or so, industrialization has had dramatic consequences. Nearly 1,800 lakes in the south of Norway are more or less devoid of fish. In half of all Sweden's lakes, stocks of fish are seriously depleted and the main salmon rivers have also suffered badly. In Canada, some 50,000 lakes are said to have been affected and fish have died out from hundreds of lakes in the Adirondacks. Acidity is measured in terms of hydrogen ion concentration (pH) and the lower the pH, the greater the acidity. Distilled water is pH7 and natural rainwater around pH5.6. As lakes drop below pH5, there is an adverse effect on fish. Trout, salmon and eel are the first to die, then perch and carp. Fish and insect-eating species like ospreys, dippers and otters also decline, partly due to the toxic effects of acidity, partly to dwindling food stocks. It is not the sulphur itself that kills the fish, but the more acid the conditions, the more aluminium is dissolved from the soil and when this enters the water it impairs the gills of the fish and interferes with their breathing. Where limestone is present in the bedrock of the lake, the acid is neutralized, which explains why other areas, while recovering similar amounts of acid rain, remain relatively unaffected.

In the late 1970s, reports began to come from Germany that the forests were dying. The trouble started with the silver fir and at first no one realized the potential extent of the problem; next the Scots pine, Norway spruce and beech began to suffer too, then the damage spread so fast that, by 1985, over half of Germany's trees were affected, one fifth of them seriously. More than two thirds of northern Germany's forest soils are acidified to a depth of one metre or more and acid rain has become a prime political issue, second only in importance to unemployment. Now trees over 6,000,000 hectares (14,900,000 acres) of Europe's forests are showing symptoms and similar damage is reported in the USSR, Eastern Europe, Canada, and in the United States in the Midwest and the high altitude areas of New England.

Below: The death of spruce trees covering Camel's Hump in Vermont is due to acid build-up. Right: The front of the Parthenon in Athens has suffered enormous damage from air pollution over the past 20 years.

Scientists differ on the exact process that kills the trees: some hold that the acid attack begins with the leaves, or needles, reducing their photosynthetic abilities and starving them of nutrients. Others maintain that the acid has robbed the soil of its nutrients, at the same time turning aluminium, which normally combines harmlessly with other soil elements, into a toxic form that attacks the roots of the trees.

Trees on hillsides, often covered with a mist heavily polluted with acid, suffered worst and in many countries, unusually high acid levels have been recorded in snow and fog over recent years. In February 1984, the snow that reached the Cairngorms in Scotland was discoloured after winds had carried it over the industrial regions of the north. It had a pH of 3.0 and trout in the fish farms of the Highlands died in their hundreds. In California, fogs with less than a pH of 3.0 are regularly recorded and occasionally reach as low as pH1.7, which is more acid than lemon juice. The environmental damage they cause has yet to be quantified.

The acid rain that helps to kill fish and trees may also have serious effects on the health of humans as toxic metals, especially aluminium, are leached from the soil and water pipes by acid and enter our drinking water. Much more research is necessary to establish the extent of the danger, but there are indications that acid rain may be implicated in chest and kidney disease and in the development of Alzheimer's Disease, which is now the fourth-biggest killer of the elderly in America.

Since the immense threat posed by sulphur dioxide has been recognized, most countries have taken steps to reduce the emissions from power stations. Some have also acted to limit emissions of nitrogen dioxide, the other major source of acid rain, but with eight times as many cars on the roads as there were 40 years ago, more and more roads carving through country areas and circling towns, and ever more cars crowding into cities, the harmful effects of pollution increase year by year. Acid rain eats into stone, brick, paper and rubber. It damages car tyres and rare books in the world's most prestigious libraries. Priceless frescoes are bubbling in the Italian art city of Florence. In Venice, heavily polluted by the nearby industrial zone, the stonework of the magnificent buildings is crumbling. The Acropolis of Athens, built nearly 2,400 years ago, has suffered worse damage in the past couple of decades than in all the rest of its history. Britain's ancient cathedrals, preserved intact for centuries, are now being eaten away by acid. In Chicago in 1986, the annual cost of damage to buildings is estimated at $45 for every single resident.

Most countries still fight shy of the measures that might be necessary to combat pollution effectively. Catalytic converters, which cut harmful emissions considerably when fitted to exhaust pipes, will be mandatory on new cars within the EEC from 1992, but environmental pressure groups point out that it will be several years before the benefits of this change are felt. In any case, converters cannot solve the problem alone. They have been compulsory in the United States since 1983, together with limits for car generated nitrogen oxides and hydrocarbons but any gains have been cancelled out by the sheer volume of traffic in a country with sprawling towns and minimal public transport. 'Green' supporters insist that far more dramatic measures, such as restrictions on cars in cities, taxes related to fuel economy and a complete rethink of public transport will be essential.

Below: A coal-fired power station in West Germany; burning fossil fuels causes acid rain. Right: Trees in the Black Forest have died in their thousands.

Deforestation

Every year more than 100,000 square kilometres (39,000 square miles) of tropical forest is destroyed. The rate of destruction varies from country to country but in West Africa, some 35,000 square kilometres are lost every year. At the current rate of clearance, India's forests may have disappeared altogether by the year 2000 and those of Amazonia could follow them within the first quarter of the 21st century. In South America, trees have been cleared for cattle ranching, to supply the enormous United States meat market at lower prices than home-produced beef. In Africa and south-east Asia, logging is big business, to supply the demand for hardwood in western countries. There are also widespread clearances for agriculture, as the developing countries struggle to feed their growing populations. Trees are felled, the useful timber removed and the remains burned, then the ash is used as agricultural fertilizer. As more farmers move into the cleared area, the demand for wood for fuel increases and yet more trees are felled.

The poor countries are often resentful of any attempted interference, claiming that they need to exploit all their natural resources for the benefit of their people. However, deforestation can have serious consequences for the very

Below: The destruction of the rain forest in countries like Brazil threatens the way of life of the native Indians who live there. Right: A jungle settlement in Brunei protected by a tropical rain forest canopy.

people it aims to help. In many countries, people have been encouraged to migrate to deforested areas and cultivate them, only to find themselves marooned in what has turned into an arid wasteland, incapable of providing them with food, let alone a livelihood. Forest soil is poor and once the protection of trees is removed, it is at the mercy of fierce sun and torrential rain. When the binding action of tree roots is destroyed, topsoil washes away and the ground soon becomes infertile. An experiment in the Amazon basin demonstrated that an annual rainfall of 215 cm (85 inches) will only wash away half a ton of soil per acre from forest soil but once the trees disappear, 45 tons is removed.

Where the ground slopes, rain that would once have been held in the ground below the trees washes down into rivers, causing the waters to rise and contributing to flooding of low-lying land. The high levels of the Amazon in 1988 resulted in widespread flooding, and the vast deforestation of the Himalayas had repercussions hundreds of kilometres away. Deforestation is also likely to contribute to the problems of global warming. Burning rainforests release hundreds of millions of tons of carbon dioxide,

adding to the 'greenhouse effect', which could mean catastrophic floods in the next century.

Scientists estimate that the rainforests contain 2,500,000 plant and tree species and that at the current rate of destruction, we could be losing 10,000 a year. Plants found in the rainforest have already been of inestimable benefit to mankind; perhaps a quarter of the medicines we buy from the chemist are based on compounds derived from these plants. Many more remain to be identified and put to use, either in the cure of diseases or developed as new sources of food.

Conservationists argue for strict international regulations on imports of hardwoods, large-scale tree-planting programmes and more pressure for international agreements on management of the remaining rainforests — even then, they say, it may never be possible to repair the harm already done.

Below: Trees are felled and the stumps burned to clear the ground for cattle grazing. Right: Yet another area of rain forest is cleared in Brazil; conservationists are pressing for more controls.

Index

Page numbers in *italic* refer to the illustrations

Aberfan, *34-5*, 35
acid rain, 182-4, *182-5*
Adair, Red, 172
Adelaide , 170
Adirondacks, 182
Africa, 88-91, 92, 178, 186
AIDS, 92-3, *92-3*
air disasters, 138-48, *138-49*
Alabama, 82, 83
Alamogordo, 52
Alaska, 32, *32*, 126, *126-7*
Alberta, 35
Alyeska Pipeline Company, 126
Amazonia, 186, 188
Amoco Cadiz, 125, *125*
Anchorage, 32, *32*
Anderson, Warren, 106
Andes, 27
Andhra Pradesh, 86
Angola, 89
Antarctica, 176, *176-7*, 180
anti-semitism, 48-50, 68
Apollo One, 110, *110-11*
Arctic, 176
Argentina, 115
Arkansas, 72, 76
Arkansas River, 76
Armenia, 30, *30-1*
Armero, 18
Arno, river, 78
Asia, 74, 186
Atentique, 28
Athens, *183*, 184
Atlantic Ocean, 130-3, 138
atmosphere, 176-84, *176-85*, 188
atom bombs, 52-4, *52-5*
Auckland, 74
Auschwitz, 49
Australia, 13, 170, *170-1*

Baltz, Stephen, 140
Bangkok, 180
Bangladesh, 86, *87*, 180
BBC, 91
Beauvais, 138
Beirut, *60-3*, 61-2
Belgium, 42, 57, 116, *116*, 136
Belsen, 50
Belzec, 49
Bengal, Bay of, 86
Bhopal, 106, *106-7*
Biafra, 56-7, *56-7*
Big Thompson Canyon, 84
Biloxi, Mississippi, *84*
Birkenau, 50
Black Death, 68-9, *68-9*
Black Forest, *185*
Boccaccio, Giovanni, 68
Bogota, 35
Boston, 80, 162
Boyd, John, 148
Bradford, 115-16, *115*
Brandenburg, Kentucky, 82
Brazil, 166, *166-7*, *186*, *189*
Britain: acid rain, 182, 184; AIDS, 92; air disasters, 138, 147-8, *147-9*; Black Death, 68; and Cambodia, 58; Depression, 99-101, *101*; fires, 158, *158-9*, 172; flu epidemic, 74; football tragedies, *114-17*, 115-16; greenhouse effect, 178, 180; and the Holocaust, 48, 50; and the Irish famine, 70; mining accidents, 163-4; rail disasters, 150-2, *150-2*; sea disasters, 130, 133, 136, *136-7*; storms,

84; thalidomide, 102-3; *Torrey Canyon*, 124, *124*; Windscale accident, *118*, 119; World War I, 42-4
Brittany, 125, *125*
Brooklyn, 140, *140-1*
Brown, Robert, 109
Brunei, *187*
bubonic plague, 69
Bulgaria, 46
bush fires, 170, *170-1*

Cairngorms, 184
Cairo, Illinois, 76
California, 73, 88, 93, 122, 184
California, Gulf of, 20
Californian, 132
Cambodia, 58, *58-9*
Camille, Hurricane, 84, *84*
Canada, 35, 50, 70-1, 80, 82, 180, 182
carbon dioxide, 178, 180, 188
Caribbean, 14-15
Caron, Lieutenant, 52-4
Carpathia, 132
Carrier, Jean-Baptiste, 41
Carter, Jimmy, 18
Caruso, Enrico, 20
Catholic church, 38, 56, 57, 104
Catorce, 152
Cemetery Hill, Yungay, 26, *26*
Centers for Disease Control, 92, 93
Central America, 80-1
Chad, 89
Chaffee, Roger, 110
Challenger space shuttle, 112-13, *112-13*
Charles II, King, 158
Chatsworth, Illinois, 150
Chelmno, 49
chemical accidents, 104-6, *104-7*
Chemie Grünenthal, 102
Chengchou, 75
Chernobyl, 119, *120-1*
Cherry, Illinois, 163
Chicago, 160, *160-1*, 184
Chimbote, 26, 27
China: flu epidemic, 74; Peking massacre, 64-5, *64-5*; Yellow River floods, 75, *75*
chlorofluorocarbons (CFCs), 176, *177*, 178
Choloma, 80
Churchill, Sir Winston, 46
Cimabue, 78, *79*
Cincinnati, *82*
Ciparis, Auguste, 17
Ciudad Guzman, 28
climate, greenhouse effect, 178-80
Cockatoo, 170
Cocoanut Grove, Boston, 162, *162*
Colima, 28
Colombia, 18, 35
Colorado, 73
Committee of Public Safety, 40
Communist Party (Soviet Union) 46
Compère-Leandre, Léon, 15
concentration camps, 49-50
Connecticut, 80
Cornwall, 124-5
Cuba, 134
Cunard, 132, 133
cyclones, 86

dams, bursting, 122, *122-3*
deforestation, 186-8, *186-9*
Delacroix, Eugène, *40*
Denmark, 120
Depression, 73, 96, *98-101*, 99-101
Dillon, Robert, 61
dioxin, 104-5
Distillers' Company, 102
Donatello, 79
Dorset, 68
drought, 88-91
drugs, thalidomide, 102-3, *102-3*
Druzes, 62
Dublin, New Hampshire, *81*
Duncan, Kelly, 144
Dust Bowl, 72-3, *72-3*, 88

earthquakes, 20-30, *20-31*
East Germany, 120
Egypt, 180
English Channel, 13
Enola Gay, 52
Environmental Protection Agency (USA), 176, 180
epidemics, 74, *74*, 92-3, *92-3*
Eritrea, 91
Ethiopia, 88-91, *89-91*
European Economic Community (EEC), 176, 178, 184
explosions, 163-4, 172-3
Exxon Valdez ,126

famines: Biafra, 56-7, *56-7*; Dust Bowl, 72-3, *72-3*; Ireland, 70-1, *70-1*; Sahel, 88-91, *89-91*
'Fat Boy', 52, 54
Ferdinand II, King of Aragon, 38
Fifi, Hurricane, 80-1, *81*
Finland, 120
Fiorelli, Giuseppe, 8
fires and explosions, 158-72, *158-73*
flagellants, 68, *68*
floods, 75-9, *75-9*, 84, 86, *87*
Florence, 78-9, *78-9*, 184
Florida, 80
flu epidemic, 74, *74*
Food and Agriculture Organization, 91
Food and Drug Administration (USA), 102
football tragedies, *114-17*, 115-16
Ford, Henry, 71
France: *Amoco Cadiz* disaster, 125, *125*; Black Death, 68; R101 disaster, 138, *139*; rail disasters, 150; French Revolution, 40-1, *40-1*; World War I, 42
Frank, Alberta, 35

Galveston, Texas, 84, *85*
Galway, *70*
Gambier, Mount, 170
gas attacks, 42, *44*
gas chambers, 49
Geldof, Bob, 91, *91*
Georgia, 82, 83, 88
Germany: acid rain, 182, *184*; Black Death, 68; Depression, 101, *101*; *Hindenburg* disaster, 138; Holocaust, 48-50, *48-51*; sinks *Lusitania*, 133; World War I, 42-4
Ghetti, Professor, 105
Ghiberti, 78, 79

Goebbels, Josef, *50*
Gorbachev, Mikhail, 30, 120, 154
Great Plain (China), 75, *75*
Great Plains (North America), 72-3
greenhouse effect, 178-80, *178-80*, 188
Gresford Colliery, 164
Grissom, Gus, 110
Grosse Island, 71
Guadalajara, 152
Guerrero, 28
Guin, Alabama, 82
Guyana, 108-9, *108-9*

Haig, Field Marshal Sir Douglas, 44
Harris, Don, 109
Hazlitt, William, 40-1
Herald of Free Enterprise, 136, *136-7*
Herculaneum, 8, 10
Heysel Stadium, 116, *116*
Hillsborough, 116, *117*
Himalayas, 188
Hindenburg, 138, *138*
Hirohito, Emperor, 54
Hiroshima, 52-4, *54-5*
Hitler, Adolf, 46, 48, *48*, 101
Hoffman La Roche, 104
Holland, 57
Holloway, *101*
Holocaust, 48-50, *48-51*
Honan, 75
Honduras, 80-1, *81*
Hong Kong, 32, *33*
Honshu, 86
Hoover, Herbert, 96, 99
Hoovervilles, *98*, 99
Huaraz, 27
Huascaran, Mount, 26
Hungary, 46
hurricanes, 80-1, *81*, 84, *84-5*

Ibo tribe, 56
Ibrox Park, *114*, 115
Idaho, 18, 122, 164-5
Illinois, 76, 150, 163
India, 106, *106-7*, 178, 186
Indian Ocean, 13, 86
Indiana, 83
Indonesia, 13
influenza, 74, *74*
Inquisition, 38, *38-9*
International Commission on Hygiene, 74
International Ice Patrol, 132
Iowa, 73
Ireland, 70-1, *70-1*, 74
Iroquois Theatre, Chicago, 160, *160-1*
Isabella, Queen of Castile, 38
Islamic Jehad Organisation, 61
Israel, 61
Italy: acid rain, 184; Black Death, 68; bursting dams, 122, *122-3*; Florence floods, 78-9, *78-9*; Pompeii, 8; Seveso disaster, 104-5, *104-5*
Iwo Jima, 52

Jalisco, 28
Japan: Hiroshima, 52-4; rail disasters, 152, *153*; Tokyo earthquake, 24-5, *24-5*; typhoons, 86
Jarvis, Greg, 112

Jasper, Alabama, 82-3
Java, 13
Jews, 38, 48-50, *48-51*, 68
Joelma Building, São Paulo, 166, *166-7*
Johnston, David, 18
Johnstown, Pennsylvania, 122
Jones, James Warren, 108-9, *108*
Jonestown, 108-9, *108-9*
Juventus football club, 116

Kaifong, 75
Kansas, 73
Kellogg, Idaho, 164-5, *164-5*
Kelly, Dorothy, 143
Kelsey, Dr Frances, 102
Kennedy, Edward, 57
Kennedy Airport, New York, 140, 147-8
Kennedy Space Center, 110
Kentucky, 82, 83, *83*
Khmer Rouge, 58, *58*
Kiev, 120
KLM, 143
Kokura, 54
Komarov, Vladimir, *111*
Korean Airlines, 146, *146*
Korem, 91
Krakatoa, *12-13*, 13, 176
Kristallnacht, 48

Lakehurst, New Jersey, 138
landslides, 32-5, *32-5*
Las Palmas airport, 143
Las Vegas, 168, *168-9*
Le Baker, Geoffrey, 68
Lebanon, *60-3*, 61-2
Leninakan, 30
Leonardo da Vinci, 78
Li Peng, 64
Lilienthal, David, *53*
Lima, 115
'Little Boy', 52, *55*
Live Aid, 91
Liverpool football club, 116
Lockerbie, 147-8, *147-9*
Loire, river, 41
Lon Nol, 58
London, 68, 101, 158, *158-9*, 180
Long Island, 80
Los Angeles, 20, 178
Los Rodeos airport, 143
Louis XVI, King of France, 40, *41*
Louisiana, 76, 84
Lusitania, 133, *133*
Lynmouth, 84

McAuliffe, Christa, 112
McNair, Ronald, 112
Madrid, 38
Makalle, 91
Manhattan Project, 52
Mannington, *163*, 164
Marat, Jean Paul, 40
Marie Antoinette, Queen, 40
Martinique, 14-15
Mauthausen, 50
Melbourne, 170
Mendocino, Cape, 20
Mexico, 152
Mexico City, 28, *28-9*, 178
MGM Grand Hotel, 168, *168-9*
Michaocan, 28
Milan, 104
mining accidents, 163-5, *163-5*
Minnesota, 73, 76
Mississippi, 84

Mississippi river, 76, *76-7*, 88
Missouri, 73, 76
Monarch of Bermuda, 134
Mondane, 150
Monongah, West Virginia, 163
Montana, 18, 73, 88
Montpelier, Vermont, 76
Montreal, 71, 80
Montreal Protocol, 176
Morrison, Herb, 138
Morro Castle, 134, *134-5*
Moscow, 46
Mozambique, 89
Muslims, 61

Nader, Ralph, 102
Nagasaki, *52*, 54
Nagoya, 86
Nantes, 41
Naples, 8
NASA, 110-13
Nazis, 48-50
Nebraska, 73
Nevada del Ruiz volcano, 18, *18-19*
New England, 72, 80, 182
New Hampshire, *81*
New London, Connecticut, 80
New Mexico, 52, 73
New Orleans, 74, 76
New York, 71, 80, *99*, 140, *140-1*, 180
New York and Cuba Mail Steamship Company, 134
New Zealand, 74
Niagara, 74
Nigeria, 56-7, *56-7*
Nordhausen, 50
North Carolina, 88
North China Herald, 75
North Dakota, 73, 88
North Sea, 172
Norway, 120, 182
Nottingham Forest football club, 116
nuclear accidents, *118-21*, 119-20

Occidental Petroleum, 172
Ohio, 76, 82, 83
Ohrdruf, 50
oil spills, 124-6, *124-7*
Ojukwu, Colonel Emeka, 56-7
Okinawa, 52
Oklahoma, 72, 73
Onizuka, Ellison, 112
Oppenheimer, J. Robert, *53*
Oregon, 84
Osaka, 86
ozone hole, 176, *176-7*

P&O, 136
Pakistan, 86
Palestine, 50
Palestine Liberation Organization, 61
Pan Am, 143, 147-8
Paris, 40-1, *74*
Parker, Andrew, 136
Pass Christian, Mississippi, 84
Passchendaele, battle of, *42*, 44
Peking, 64-5, *64-5*, 180
Pelée, Mont, 14-15, *14*
Pennsylvania, 122
People's Liberation Army, 64-5
Pepys, Samuel, 158
Peru, 26-7, *26-7*, 115
Phnom Penh, 58

Piper Alpha, 172, *172-3*
Piranesi, Giambattista, *9*
plague, 68-9, *68-9*
Pliny the Younger, 8
Pol Pot, 58
Poland, 46, 48, 50, 120
pollution, acid rain, 182-4, *182-5*
Pompeii, 8-10, *10-11*
potato famine, Ireland, 70
Potomac River, 144, *144-5*
Potsdam Declaration, 52
Pravda, 30
Prince William Sound, 126

Quebradablanca Canyon, 35
Quintinshill, 152

R101, 138, *139*
rail disasters, 150-4, *150-5*
rainforests, 186-8, *186-9*
rats, 69
Reagan, Ronald, 61, 62, 113, 146
Red Army, 46
Red Cross, 76, 81, 116
Resnek, Judith, 112
Rhode Island, 80
Rio de Janeiro, 35
Riordan, J.J., 96
Robespierre, Maximilien, 40, 41
Rockefeller, John D., 96
Rogers, William, 113
Rome, 180
Roosevelt, Franklin D., 101
Royal Scots, 152
Rumania, 46
Ryan, Leo, 108-9

Sahel, 88-91
St Francis Dam, 122
St Helens, Mount, 17-18, *17*
St Lawrence River, 71
St Pierre, 14-17, *14*
Sakhalin Island, 146
Salyut One, 110
San Andreas fault, 20, 23, 76
San Francisco, 13, 20-3, *20-3*, 92, 108
San Pedro Sula, 80
São Paulo, 166, *166-7*
São Tomé, 56, 57
Scandinavia, 176, 182
Scarlatti, 78
Scilly Isles, 124
Scobee, Francis, 112
Scotland, 147-8, 150, 152, 172, 184
sea disasters, 130-6, *130-7*
Senghenydd mine, 163-4
Seveso, 104-5, *104-5*
Sheffield, 116
Sheridan, Martin, 162
Shiite Muslims, 61
Sidney, 180
Sixtus IV, Pope, 38
Skutnik, Lennie, 144
Smith, Captain Edward, 130, *131*
Smith, Michael, 112
Sobibor, 49
Somme, battle of the, 42
Sop, Julius, 132
South America, 108-9, 186
South Australia, 170
South Dakota, 73
South Fork Dam, 122
Soviet Union: Armenian earthquake, 30, *30-1*; Chernobyl accident, 119, 120,

120-1; Holocaust, 50; Korean Airlines disaster, 146; rail disasters, 154, *154-5*; space programme, 110, *111*; Stalin's purges, 46, *46-7*; World War II, 48, 52
Soyuz Eleven, 110, *111*
space shuttle, 112-13, *112-13*
space travel, 110-13, *110-13*
Spain, 38, *38-9*, 74
Spitak, 30
Stalin, Josef, 46
Staten Island, 71, 140, *141*
Steinbeck, John, 73
storms, 80-6, *81-7*
Straus, Isador, 132
Sudan, 89
Sugar Valley, Georgia, 83
suicides, Jonestown, 108-9, *108-9*
Sumatra, 13
The Sunday Times, 102
Sweden, 120, 182
Syracuse University, 147-8
Syria, 61

Tay Bridge, 150, *150-1*
Tenerife, 143, *143*
Tennessee, 83, 88
Teton Dam, 122
Texas, 72, 73, 84
thalidomide, 102-3, *102-3*
Three Mile Island, *119*, 120
Tiananmen Square, Peking, 64-5, *64-5*
tidal waves, 13, 86
Tigre, 91
Titanic, 130-2, *130-2*
Toc, Mount, 122
Tokyo, 24-5, *24-5*, 152, *153*
Tolstoy, Count Nikolai, 46
tornados, 82-3, *82-3*
Torquemada, Tomás de, 38
Torrey Canyon, 124-5, *124*
torture, 38, *38*, 50, 58
Townsend Thoresen, 136
Transworld Airlines, 140
Treblinka, 49, 50
trees: acid rain, 182-4, *182*, *185*; deforestation, 186-8, *186-9*
Truman, Harry S., 52, 54
tsunamis, 13
Turtle Mountain, 35
typhoons, 86
typhus, 70, 71

U-boats, 133
Uffizi Gallery, Florence, 78
unemployment, 99-101
Union Carbide, 106
United Airlines, 140, *141*
United Nations, 91
United Nations Commission on Human Rights, 58
United States of America: acid rain, 182, 184; AIDS, 92-3; air disasters, 140, *140-1*, 144, *144-5*, 146, 147-8; Alaska oil spill, 126, *126-7*; bursting dams, 122; and Cambodia, 58; and deforestation, 186; Depression, 96, *98-9*, 99-101; Dust Bowl, 72-3, *72-3*, 88; fires, 160-2, *160*, 168, *168-9*; flu epidemic, 74; greenhouse effect, 178, 180; help for the Biafran famine, 57; *Hindenburg* disaster, 138, *138*; Hiroshima,

52-4; and the Holocaust, 48, 50; hurricanes, 86; Irish emigration to, 70-1; and the Lebanese civil war, 61-2; mining accidents, 163, *163-5*, 164-5; Mississippi floods, 76, *76-7*; *Morro Castle* disaster, 134, *134-5*; and the ozone hole, 176; rail disasters, 150; San Francisco earthquake, 20-3, *20-3*; space programme, 110-13, *110-11*; storms, 80, 82-4, *82-5*; thalidomide, 102; Three Mile Island accident, *119*, 120; *Titanic* disaster, 130-2; Wall Street Crash, 96, *96-7*; World War I, 44
Ural Mountains, 154

US Geological Survey, 18, 26
US Marines, 61, 62
US Research Council, 180

Vaiont Dam, 122, *122-3*
Valencia, 38
Venice, 184
Verdun, battle of, 42
Vermont, 76, *182*
Vespucci, Amerigo, 78
Vesuvius, Mount, 8, *8-9*, 10
Victoria, 170
Vietnam, 58, 104
Vincent, Dr Thomas, 158
volcanoes, 8-18, *8-19*

Wales, 35, 163-4
Wall Street Crash, 96, *96-7*

Warms, William, 134
Warsaw, 48, 50
Washington, 144
The Washington Post, 102
Washington State, 17
Wead, Robert, 18
Welansky, Barney, 162
West Virginia, 163, 164
White, Ed, 110
White Russians, 46
Whyte, Rev. James, 148
Wilkenson, Tom, *164*
Willmott, Robert, 134
Willow Creek, Oregon, 84
Windscale, *118*, 119
Windsor, Ontario, 82
World Bank, 88-9
World Health Organization, 92, 93

World War I, 42-4, *42-5*, 74, 133, 150
World War II, 46, 48-50, *48-51*, 52-4, 101
Wren, Christopher, 158
Wright, Frank Lloyd, 24
Wyoming, 73

Xenia, Ohio , 82

Yalta Conference, 46
Yellow River, 75, *75*
Yokohama, 24-5, *24*
Ypres, *42-3*
Yu, Emperor, 75
Yungay, 26, *26*

Zeebrugge, 136

Photographic Acknowledgements

Associated Press 33, 77 inset, 84-5, 94-5, 122, 134-5, 135 inset, 153, 160, 162, 165, 166-7 inset

Bettmann Archive 55, 146 / UPI 27, 32, 111 top

Bridgeman Art Library 79 / Bibliotheque National, Paris 41 / Guildhall Art Gallery, London 158-9 / The Louvre, Paris 40 / Museum of London 159 inset

Bruce Coleman Ltd / Robert P Carr 178, 181 / Hans Reinhard 185 / Norman Tomalin 180

Ecoscene 186-7

Mary Evans Picture Library 8, 23-3 inset, 44-5, 133, 161

Robert Harding Pictured Library 10 inset, 26, 75, 174-5, 186 inset

The John Hillelson Agency / Sygma 108-9 / Alain Nogues 87

Michael Holford 10-11

Hulton Deutsch Company 22, 35, 36-7, 39 top, 48, 50-1, 54, 69, 70, 73, 74, 100-1, 114, 124, 152

Imperial War Museum, London 42-3, 44 below, 45 below

Frank Lane Picture Agency 17 inset, 83

The Library of Congress, Washington 72

Magnum / Thomas Hopker 66-7 / Michael K Nichols 188-9, 189 right / Raghu Rai 86

Mansell Collection 14-15, 68, 132, 151 top / Illustrated London News 139

Popperfoto 134, 15 right, 21 inset, 34, 46-7, 47 inset, 50 inset, 53 top, 53 inset, 56, 57, 82, 99, 101 inset, 108 left, 116, 119, right, 123, 138, 140-1, 140-1 inset, 163, 164

Rex Features 16-17, 18, 91, 92, 93, 102-3, 112-3, 147, 149, 172-3, 179, 183 / British Nuclear Fuels 118-9 / Sipa Press title page, 19, 28, 29, 30, 59, 60, 61, 62, 63, 64, 65, 81 bottom, 89, 90, 104-5 top, 104-5 bottom, 106, 107, 112 inset, 125, 128-9, 136, 137, 142, 143, 144, 145, 168-9, 169 inset, 171 inset, 177 / Sipa Press – Novosti 121 / Today 117 top, 117 bottom, 126, 127, 148, 173 inset

Science Photo Library / Martin Dohrn 184 / Stewart Lowther 6-7 / Jerry Mason 170-1 / Nasa 176 / Townsend Dickinson 182

Frank Spooner Pictures 88 / Gamma 156-7

Syndication International 12, 24, 31, 49, 58, 76-7, 81 top, 97, 115 / The British Museum, London 9 / The Illustrated London News 20-1, 131 inset / Novosti 110

Tass / A Solovyov 154, 155 / Zufarov 120

Topham Picture Library 25, 38, 39 bottom, 78, 85 inset, 96, 98, 102 inset, 113 right, 130-1, 150-1 / NASA 111 bottom

United States Air Force 52-3

The Trustees of the Watts Gallery, Compton 71